LEVERAGING THE POWER OF SEASONS

Understanding and Taking Advantage of the Four Seasons of Life

TOYIN OBAFEMI

Copyright 2023 by Toyin Obafemi

Published by Pnuxel Consulting
toyin@pnuxelconsulting.com

CONTENTS

ACKNOWLEDGEMENTS

First and foremost, I want to give all glory and honour to God, the giver of time, life, and opportunity. Without Him, none of this would be possible.

My deepest gratitude goes to my beautiful wife, Temitope, for her unwavering support and encouragement throughout this journey. Her belief in me and this project has been a constant source of motivation. Her love and patience have been invaluable.

I would also like to thank our precious children, Oreofe and Inioluwa, for being a source of inspiration. Their joy and curiosity remind me of the importance of living in the present and making the most of every moment.

I am also deeply grateful to Adewobi Adebanjo for going out of his way to design the cover for this book. You have always been reliable. Thank you!

Chapter One

EMBRACE THE SEASONS, HARVEST YOUR SUCCESS

Welcome to the inspiring exploration of life's seasons, where every twist and turn holds profound wisdom. Just as nature orchestrates its changing phases, our lives follow a pattern of four distinct seasons. Through relatable stories and simple explanations, we're about to unravel this concept, one layer at a time.

Imagine watching the world outside your window. Trees go from bare branches to lush green, and then their leaves transform into a vivid symphony of autumn colours. This dance of change isn't just a coincidence. It's a clue that nature gives us about the rhythm of life. It is a constant reminder that change is an integral part of life. Just like the earth goes through different seasons, our lives also flow in cycles of change. When you think about it, our experiences align with these natural changes. Just as winter yields to spring, challenges give way to opportunities.

But what if I told you that these seasonal transitions aren't just about the weather? They're also an insightful reflection of our lives. Picture life as a journey through four unique seasons: Winter, Spring, Summer, and Autumn. Each season comes with its distinct characteristics and teachings. Just as winter can be a time of harshness, it's a period for growth through adversity. Spring, known as the seed time, represents opportunities. Summer, the season of nurturing, parallels the growth and progress we experience. Finally, Autumn marks the time of harvest, where we reap what we've sown.

EMBRACING CHANGE AND GROWTH

Here's the beautiful part: these seasons aren't just for some people. They're universal. Like the sun rising and setting for everyone, we all go through these phases. It's easy to think that someone else life is all Spring and Summer, but remember, even the sun has to face its dawning. Knowing that everyone experiences these changes makes the journey relatable and reassuring. **No one is immune to life's challenges, just as no one is exempt from its blessings.** It's easy to believe that others have it easier, but the truth is we all experience these seasons to varying degrees. Knowing this can provide comfort in tough times and encourage us to appreciate the good ones.

Change is constant in life and must be embraced rather than resisted. I understand that change can be scary, especially when you are transitioning into the winter, sometimes referred to as the night, but as much as we do not like this change, it is incredibly powerful as it comes with its opportunities. This is why I am writing this book to you so you can take advantage of the seasons and not bury your head in sadness and sorrow.

Each season has its purpose and brings us opportunities for growth and transformation. Just as winter brings the chance to endure and overcome hardships, it prepares us for the abundance of spring. By accepting change and understanding its role in our lives, we open ourselves to learning and progress. **Warriors are not made in the bedroom but on the field and at the war front.**

A young boy found himself in an unexpected situation. As he entered a compound, a big dog charged towards him with an intensity that sent his heart racing. Fear fueled his instincts as he sprinted toward the nearest escape - a tall fence. With adrenaline surging, he leapt over the fence with a vigour he never knew he had. Once safe on the other side, he looked back at the formidable barrier he had just cleared. It struck him that he might have never believed himself capable of such a feat without the pursuit of the dog.

Similarly, the challenges we face in life, like the unexpected appearance of the dog, can seem daunting. Yet, they hold the potential to bring out the very best in us. Just as the boy discovered hidden strength within himself during that pursuit, we too often unearth incredible abilities and resilience when faced with hardships. These challenges push us to tap into resources we didn't know we possessed, revealing depths of strength we might have never acknowledged. This is what I call self-discovery, and it is the most valuable journey of our lives—the journey of knowing who we are.

The earth's shape explains why we have day and night. When one side faces the sun, it's day there; when it turns away, it's night- this movement is called the earth's rotation, which means that the earth is rotating about its axis. Also, the earth moves around the sun, leading to seasons- this is referred to as the revolutionary movement of the planet Earth. It takes the Earth one year to complete this motion around the sun, which explains the year's diverse seasons. Is this not beautiful?

God created the seasons, the day and night, which shall not cease as long as the earth exists. *"While the earth remains, seedtime and harvest, cold and heat, summer and winter, day and night, shall not cease."*(1) This makes sense because the seasons, the day and night, will not cease as long as the earth continues to move. This also applies to humans, as we are not immune to change: there will always be changes in our lives as long as we exist on earth. The difficult time will come, and we can do nothing to stop it. Everyone will have their dose of it, but the good news is that it does not last forever. Every winter opens doors to spring, so if you are going through a difficult time, I encourage you to hold on a little more because it is just for a time. **Weeping endures for a night, but joy comes in the morning.**(2)

Nothing is immune to change except God. Whether for good or bad, change is inevitable. Instead of consistently praying for good things, pray for the wisdom and courage to handle whatever comes your way, as both the good and the bad will inevitably cross your path.

As we embark on this incredible journey through life's seasons, remember one thing: we can't change the seasons themselves. **No matter how hard we try, tearing up a calendar or turning back our clocks won't change nature's course. But there's one thing we can change: ourselves.** We can adapt, learn, and grow with each season. In the chapters ahead, we'll delve deep into each season's lessons, revealing practical strategies to take advantage of the seasons. So, gear up for a remarkable adventure. We're about to explore the power of seasons, unveiling their treasures to transform how we view our lives and ultimately achieve great success.

SETTING THE TONE FOR THE LESSONS AHEAD

Every life is a story written across the pages of time. It's a tale of spring's rejuvenation, summer's growth, autumn's harvest, and winter's reflection. We all experience these seasons, not only in nature but within the essence of our very existence. This book explores these four life seasons, a journey through their differences, challenges, and extraordinary opportunities.

Life is not static; it's a dynamic progression. Just as the seasons transform the world around us, we evolve in unison with the changing tides of our lives. Our understanding of these seasons and our ability to leverage them can shape the course of our journey to great success.

In this book, we'll embark on a voyage through these seasons, uncovering the wisdom they hold. Each chapter offers a unique perspective, helping you embrace the rhythm of life's seasons. Whether you're navigating the hardships of winter, seizing the opportunities of spring, nurturing and protecting in your season of growth, or reaping the rewards of your labour, these pages will be a valuable guide.

It's great to recognise that challenges only last for a while. As winter gives way to spring, difficulties pave the path for opportunities; therefore, cultivate a positive mindset and develop the wisdom to recognise these openings.

This book will teach you how to protect your growth and progress, offering insights into nurturing and safeguarding your dreams. It will encourage you to take responsibility for your harvest and inspire you to understand the significance of learning to enjoy the fruits of your labour.

As we embark on this journey, remember that every word you read is a step closer to a more profound understanding of your life's seasons. You are the leading character in this story, and it's time to embrace the seasons, harvest your success, and live your life's most meaningful chapters.

The lessons within these pages aren't just ink on paper; they are the voices of experience and the wisdom of those who've walked the path before you. So, turn the page and let's begin this incredible journey through life's seasons.

Welcome to a transformative exploration of life's seasons; welcome to the journey of a lifetime.

.

Chapter Two

NAVIGATING THE WINTER OF CHALLENGES

"Pain is temporary. It may last a minute, or an hour, or a day, or a year, but eventually it will subside and something else will take its place. If I quit, however, it lasts forever. That surrender, even the smallest act of giving up, stays with me. So when I feel like quitting, I ask myself, which would I rather live with?" - Lance Armstrong

Imagine stepping out into the biting cold, feeling the shiver that races down your spine. With its frosty touch, winter symbolises life's tough times, much like the unexpected challenges that life throws at us. Just as the boy illustrated in the previous chapter encountered a fierce dog, we too can face unexpected difficulties – losing a loved one, financial struggles, economic recessions, famine or setbacks in our plans- the list continues. These setbacks are not new, as they are in cycles. People will lose their jobs, and it will be like it is the end of the world and sooner or later, there will be increased job opportunities. We do not have control over this because life is in seasons and cycles. Though we do not have control over the season, we have control over our lives.

Pause and think about it: Do we pray for winter not to come, or do we petition the government to halt its arrival? The truth is winter is inevitable. Our response, then, shapes how we navigate it. We don't avert winter; we prepare for it. We gather warm clothes and make arrangements to ensure our well-being through the season. In essence, we handle the winter.

Similarly, when life's challenges arise, you must choose how you respond to them. You should handle your winter with strength and courage. As you read this passage, you can tell yourself, **"I handle my winter because I have what it takes."**

The Creator has given us what it takes to go through the winter of our lives. If He allowed the winter without providing us with what it takes to go through it, then He is not fair, but the good news is that you have all it takes to make greatness out of your winter. Apostle Paul rightly affirmed this when he said, **"The temptations [winter] in your life are no different from what others experience. And God is faithful. He will not allow the temptation [winter] to be more than you can stand. When you are tempted, he will show you a way out so that you can endure."**(3) (emphasis mine)

Remember that the brilliance of gold is brought out by heat. Your hidden potential is waiting for the winter to expose it. Here's the lesson: how you handle winter mirrors how you should take life's challenges. Rather than simply pray to avoid difficulty or lament its arrival, you should actively prepare yourself to navigate it with strength and determination. Just as you gather winter coats and warm scarves, you should harness your inner resources – resilience, adaptability, and unwavering resolve. Winter teaches you that you possess the ability to not only survive but thrive despite the chill.

So, the next time you encounter difficult times, remember the lesson of the winter: it's not about evading the cold but about embracing your ability to endure and flourish within it. Say to yourself, **"I am prepared, and I will handle it."** With this mindset, you'll approach challenges not with fear but with the confidence that you have the strength to weather any storm, and you will. When you come out on the other side, your story will impact and help others, just as the great teacher told Peter to help others when he has gone through the trial. **"Simon, stay on your toes. Satan has tried his best to separate all of you from me, like chaff from wheat. Simon, I've prayed for you in**

particular that you not give in or give out. When you have come through the time of testing [winter], turn to your companions and give them a fresh start."(4) (emphasis mine)

WINTER DOES NOT LAST FOREVER SO DOES HARDSHIP

Was there a year when it was winter all through? Probably not. Winter does not last forever; it has its time limit and expiry date, which is good news. If you are going through a difficult time, I am glad to inform you that it will only last for a while as it has its expiry date and will break. As winter gives room to spring, so will your difficulties give way to opportunities, so be encouraged and take advantage of the season you find yourself.

As the winter prepares nature for spring renewal, life's difficulties prepare you for growth and opportunities. You might not have control over your challenges, just as you can't control when winter arrives. But just as the boy jumped over the fence, you can rise above your challenges. Instead of fearing winter, you can see it as a chance to shine, showcase your hidden abilities, and learn lessons that will serve you well in all seasons.

Moreso, I am afraid to tell you that the opportunities that follow the winter do not last forever. It also has an expiry date. This is why you should not waste the springs- you should instead take advantage of them. How you handle the spring will determine your comfort next winter. We will delve more into this subject in the next chapter, and the story of Joseph stands out to drive home this lesson.

SEIZING THE SPRING: THE JOSEPH PRINCIPLE

The story of Joseph, a figure from ancient times, beautifully illustrates this principle of seizing the spring, thus preparing to weather the winter. Joseph's life journey was filled with challenges and unexpected turns. Sold into slavery by his brothers, he found himself in Egypt, where his talent for interpreting dreams eventually caught the attention of Pharaoh.

Pharaoh had a dream of fat and slim cows, symbolising years of plenty followed by seven years of famine. In essence, it was a premonition of a coming winter after a bountiful spring.

Joseph's wisdom in advising Pharaoh to store away twenty per cent of the harvest instead of merely relying on prayer to avert the famine is a profound lesson. While prayer is undoubtedly a valuable tool, usually answered prayers come in the form of wisdom and strategy to navigate through challenging times.

Consider the words of the Great Teacher regarding prayer, where He encourages us not only to ask but also to seek and knock. "**Keep on asking, and you will receive what you ask for. Keep on seeking, and you will find. Keep on knocking, and the door will be opened to you.**"(5)

This threefold approach is a strategic framework; I refer to it as the **ASK strategy**. The 'A' stands for Ask, S stands for Seek, while K stands for Knock. In other words, prayers aren't complete until we engage in the seeking and knocking phases. Seeking and knocking symbolise the wisdom and strategy required to understand what actions we must take to obtain what we've asked for.

It's no coincidence that in the word 'ask,' we find 'ASK,' emphasising that genuine asking involves not just words but also the pursuit of wisdom and the strategic effort required to realise our desires.

Joseph did not tell them to pray, which is good, but he urged them to seize the abundance of the spring, the seven years of plenty, by storing away twenty per cent of the harvest. This strategic decision to capitalise on the opportunities presented during the spring became the lifeline that helped them endure and overcome the challenging winter of famine that came.

But why twenty per cent? Why not the more common tithe (ten per cent), or seven per cent, signifying the seven years or even less? Joseph's choice was strategic and well-calculated. Imagine if they had stored away only seven per cent of the harvest. When the famine arrived, it wouldn't have been enough to sustain the people. Even ten per cent, often associated with tithing, might have needed more buffer. Joseph's foresight and insight allowed him to recommend a more significant twenty per cent. This mathematical decision ensured there was an ample surplus to not only endure but thrive during the approaching winter.

In life, just like in Joseph's story, it's essential to be strategic when managing opportunities in preparation for difficult times ahead. By having foresight and insight, you can make well-planned decisions that set you up for success during the springs and winters of life. In the next chapter, we'll delve deeper into this concept of seizing the spring, exploring practical strategies to make the most of life's opportunities and setting ourselves up for resilience and abundance during the winters.

FINDING COMFORT IN YOUR DARKEST MOMENTS

As we venture through life's seasons, there are moments when we find ourselves in the valleys of challenges. These times can feel like wandering through darkness, but they bring to mind the timeless words of Psalms 23– a passage that holds a special place in my heart. My mum used to guide us through this scripture, and I have found its wisdom distilled into my being with time. Interestingly, I could recite this passage in multiple languages. She made us learn it, and I am grateful she did: what an amazing mother.

Psalms 23 starts with the profound declaration, **"The Lord is my shepherd, I shall not want."** It paints a vivid picture of the Divine as a caring shepherd who guides and provides for us, much like a shepherd tends to his flock. But the Psalm does not sugarcoat life or promise an existence free of valleys. Instead, it assures us that we are not alone, even in our darkest moments.

Consider the vivid imagery in the verse – **"He makes me lie down in green pastures."** This phrase reminds us of moments of tranquillity and abundance. But the Psalm did not stop there. It continues, **"Though I walk through the valley of the shadow of death, I will fear no evil, for you are with me; your rod and your staff, they comfort me."** This acknowledges that we will inevitably journey through challenging valleys, which the Psalmist called the valley of the shadow of death.

The message is clear: we can't evade these valleys, but we can find solace in the presence of the Divine, beautifully symbolised by the shepherd's rod and staff. These represent guidance and protection. The verse reassures us that we are not alone, even in the darkest valleys; we are comforted, guided, and protected. As one of Harvey Dent's quotes says, **"The night is darkest just before the dawn. And I promise you, the dawn is coming."** John Green drops his own words, **"The darkest nights produce the brightest stars."**

More importantly, God has given you all it takes to go through the darkest moments. Just as winter's hardships prepare you for spring's growth, the valleys of life shape you, fostering growth, resilience, and a deeper understanding of your inner strength.

Remember, as you navigate life's seasons, these valleys are part of the journey, not a detour. The lessons learned in these challenging times are invaluable, shaping you into stronger, more resilient individual who can express their hidden treasures and help others.

Your journey to discovering the insights in the seasons of life had just begun. You are in to gain outstanding value for your time.

FINDING STRENGTH THROUGH THE FLAMES

Amidst life's trials and tribulations, we can find solace in these words: **"When you pass through the waters, I will be with you; and through the rivers, they shall not overflow you. When you walk through the fire,**

you shall not be burned, nor shall the flame scorch you."(6) These profound words reassure us that we are not alone as we journey through the symbolic waters and fires of adversity.

To illustrate this promise, let us turn to the story of three remarkable individuals – Shadrach, Meshach, and Abednego – who faced the scorching flames of a fiery furnace. King Nebuchadnezzar ordered these three men to worship an idol, and when they refused, in his rage, he condemned them to a burning fiery furnace heated seven times hotter than usual. We should have thought that God would aid them by preventing them from entering the fire- the reverse was the case. He did not prevent the fiery trial. Instead, He joined them in the furnace, standing as the fourth person among the flames. This miraculous intervention demonstrates that we may pass through the fires of hardship, but God's presence ensures we emerge unharmed and strengthened.

Subsequently, King Nebuchadnezzar, astonished by what he witnessed, acknowledged the power of the God of Shadrach, Meshach, and Abednego. This testimony serves as a testament to the unwavering presence of the Divine in our most challenging moments. Just as the fiery furnace did not consume these faithful individuals, our difficulties can refine us, leaving us stronger, better and fit for the success ahead.

STRENGTH IS FORGED IN ADVERSITY, NOT COMFORT.

Warriors are not made in the bedroom. Have you ever heard of a General or Colonel who was decorated while he spent his life in the comfort of his bedroom? This question prompts us to consider an essential truth: **warriors, whether on the battlefield or in life's struggles, are not crafted in comfort but forged in the fires of adversity.**

As the quote suggests, "Strength is forged in adversity, not comfort." To illustrate this concept further, consider the words of Carlos Castaneda: *"The basic difference between an ordinary man and a warrior is that a warrior takes everything as a challenge while an ordinary man takes everything as a blessing or a curse."* Warriors, in both the military and life itself, see challenges as opportunities for growth. They don't seek the comfort of their bedroom; instead, they venture into the battlefield of life, ready to face whatever comes their way.

Another insightful quote by Jake Remington emphasises the warrior's mindset: *"Fate whispers to the warrior, 'You cannot withstand the storm.' The warrior whispers back, 'I am the storm.'"* Warriors understand that life's storms are inevitable. They don't hide from them; they become the storm, resilient and unyielding in the face of adversity. Just as a military leader earns decorations on the battlefield, you gain wisdom and strength when facing life's challenges head-on.

As difficulties surround us in winter, remember that it's not a time to retreat to the bedroom of comfort.

Instead, it's an opportunity to embrace challenges and grow stronger. Just as the military leader is not honoured for staying in the bedroom, you are not celebrated for avoiding life's trials. The path to becoming a warrior involves facing adversity with courage and unwavering determination.

CLIMBING ON THE WINGS OF DISAPPOINTMENT TO GREAT ACHIEVEMENT: SECRETS TO NEVER BE DISAPPOINTED

Why do we often feel profoundly disappointed when adversity knocks at our door? Why do we view challenges as unwelcome guests rather than opportunities for growth and transformation? These questions lead us to a deeper understanding of our reactions to adversity and the hidden secret to avoiding disappointment.

Disappointment in the face of adversity often stems from our expectations of a smooth and comfortable life. We create mental images of a path paved with ease, without obstacles. When reality confronts these expectations, we feel let down. It's as if we've been handed a script that doesn't match the story we had written.

You are disappointed when your reality does not match your expectations. In other words, you are disappointed to the extent of your expectations.

Let's consider this in the context of believers. Many of us, driven by our faith in a loving and all-powerful God, sometimes become the worst handlers of disappointment. We may wonder, "Why is this happening to me when I've been faithful?" It's essential to understand that while God is indeed benevolent, He also allows trials to shape us and reveal the best within us. Disappointment can be especially challenging for believers who never expected adversity from a loving God.

As William Shakespeare said, *"Expectation is the root of all heartache."* Sometimes, we create our heartbreaks through expectations. Alexander Pope reminds us, *"Blessed is he who expects nothing, for he shall never be disappointed."* It's not about erasing all expectations but finding a balance between hoping for the best and understanding that life may bring unexpected challenges.

The secret to not being disappointed lies in a shift of perspective. Instead of seeing adversity obstructing our carefully planned life, we can view it as a teacher. Challenges, setbacks, and difficulties are not here to thwart us but to instruct us. They are our most incredible mentors, offering lessons that comfort and ease could never provide.

Consider it like the seed that must push through the dark, compact earth to reach the sunlight. If the seed was uncooperative, it might find this journey disappointing. Yet, this very struggle enables the seed to grow into a towering tree. Similarly, adversity is the soil through which we grow. It nurtures our resilience, determination, and character.

In life, adversity is not a flaw but a necessary thread. It is an essential part of our growth, helping us become the best versions of ourselves. Embracing this truth allows us to unlock the secret: we can face adversity without disappointment because we understand its role in our journey. It's not here to harm us but to help us evolve. Just as a seed must push through the dark, compact earth to reach the sunlight, we must face challenges to grow to our fullest potential. **Our faith is not a shield against adversity; it is the strength we draw upon to navigate it.**

So the next time adversity knocks at your door, remember that it carries the opportunity for growth and transformation. Instead of greeting it with disappointment, welcome it as a wise teacher, ready to impart invaluable lessons. As Gary Busey says, *"Pray for the best, prepare for the worst, and expect the unexpected."* In doing so, you'll find that the disappointments of adversity become the stepping stones to your most outstanding achievements.

"Disappointment is really just a term for our refusal to look on the bright side," noted Richelle E. Goodrich

ADVERSITY: A TEST OF FAITH AND CHARACTER

Life's journey is filled with unexpected twists and turns, and it's often when we least expect it that adversity knocks on our door. For many, especially those of faith, this can be profoundly challenging. It's natural to wonder why difficulties arise when we've been diligent in our devotion. But remember, even the most robust trees are tested by the storms.

The Great Teacher admonished us to build our house on the rock, not the sand, so we would stand when the storm came. Building on the rock does not allow us to evade floods and storms but makes us stand when the storm comes. Adversity tests our faith and character. **"If you faint in the day of adversity, Your strength is small."(7)**

Adversity serves as a crucible— a place where our beliefs and character are refined. Like precious metal subjected to intense heat, we emerge from the fires of adversity stronger and more resilient. **Our faith is not meant to shield us from life's challenges but to fortify us as we face them. It's the anchor we hold onto when the storms of life rage.**

The story of Job in the Bible exemplifies this truth. Job, a man of unwavering faith, faced unimaginable adversity. Despite his suffering, he held onto his faith, proclaiming, **"Though he slay me, yet will I trust in him."**(8) Job's story teaches us that faith is not the absence of adversity but the unwavering belief in God's goodness, even in the midst of trials.

The disappointment that often accompanies adversity is a human reaction to unmet expectations. God allows us to face adversity not to disappoint but to develop us. **Just as athletes must endure rigorous training to reach their full potential, we must navigate life's challenges to become the best versions of ourselves.**

In the face of adversity, faith is not passive; it is the active choice to trust and persevere. It is the belief that even in the darkest times, God is with us, shaping us and preparing us for a brighter future. So, when disappointment looms in adversity's shadow, remember that it's a temporary cloud in the grand scheme of your journey. This cloud will eventually reveal the sunshine of resilience, character, and unwavering faith.

"Friends, when life gets really difficult [winter], don't jump to the conclusion that God isn't on the job. Instead, be glad that you are in the very thick of what Christ experienced. This is a spiritual refining process, with glory just around the corner."(9) (emphasis mine)

WINTER'S LESSONS, SPRING'S PROMISE: THE CONTINUUM OF LIFE

Every season has its purpose in life, and the winter of challenges is no exception. We've explored the profound truth that adversity is not meant to break but to mould us. It's a season where the chill of disappointment can be transformed into the warmth of resilience, where the darkest nights become the backdrop for the brightest stars. As we navigate the winter, we must remember that adversity does not diminish our faith; rather, it is strengthened.

In the coming chapters, we will delve deeper into the ever-turning wheel of life's seasons. Our next stop is the spring of opportunities, a time when seeds of potential are planted. Just as the winter prepares the ground for new growth, the spring invites us to recognise and seize the budding opportunities.

As the lessons of the winter are etched into your character, you are well-equipped to embrace the challenges and triumphs that lie ahead. So, as we bid farewell to the winter of challenges, let us march onward, ready to bloom in the coming spring of opportunities.

Let's continue this journey as we move to the next chapter, **'Seizing the Spring of Opportunities,'** where we will uncover the secrets of recognising, nurturing, and harvesting the abundant opportunities that await us on this remarkable life's journey.

Chapter Three

SEIZING THE SPRING OF OPPORTUNITIES. STORYTIME!

"Opportunity is missed by most people because it is dressed in overalls and looks like work." – Thomas A. Edison

As the winter's chill gradually fades, the world comes alive with a vibrant burst of colour and energy. It's the season of spring, a time when nature herself seems to whisper the promise of new beginnings. In the same way that the barren trees of winter eventually sprout fresh leaves and blossoms, our lives are filled with growth and renewal seasons.

This chapter will focus on the spring of opportunities, a season of immense potential and transformation. Just as the earth awakens with the arrival of spring, so too can we awaken to the possibilities that lie before us. It's a time to recognise the seeds of potential in our lives, nurture them with care and determination, and ultimately reap the abundant rewards of seizing the opportunities that abound. Join me on this journey as we explore the art of recognising, embracing, and making the most of the spring seasons of our lives.

Let us start with some stories.

RECOGNISING OPPORTUNITIES

Let me introduce you to the story of Edwin C. Barnes, a man with a dream that defied convention. Barnes had one audacious goal: becoming Thomas Edison's partner. However, there was a significant hurdle on his path — he didn't have the means to travel to Edison's location, let alone impress the legendary inventor.

Against the odds, Barnes reached Edison's office and boldly declared his ambition to be Edison's business partner. Unsurprisingly, Edison refused this lofty request. Yet, something about Barnes' unwavering attitude caught Edison's attention. Instead of turning Barnes away completely, Edison offered him a humble position as a sweeper. Barnes enthusiastically accepted this seemingly menial job because he recognised the opportunity in this seeming rejection.

For the next two years, Barnes diligently swept floors while observing Edison's way of working. During this time, Edison designed a groundbreaking product called the 'Ediphone' and wanted to bring it to market. However, Edison's sales team dismissed the idea, deeming it unworkable. This is where Barnes's journey takes a remarkable turn.

Drawing from his observations and his unyielding belief in Edison's inventions, Barnes devised a plan to sell the 'Ediphone.' He presented his strategy to Edison, who, impressed by Barnes's ingenuity and determination, approved him. The plan worked and exceeded expectations, leading to the successful sales of numerous 'Ediphones.' Out of this business association grew the slogan, **'Made by Edison and installed by Barnes.'** He finally became the business partner of Edison and launched his own company, 'Edwin C. Barnes and Bros'

Barnes' determination, unwavering belief, and willingness to start small eventually led him to his dream. He didn't give up when Edison initially refused his proposal. Instead, he took on the sweeper role, confident that working closely with Edison would propel him towards his goal. Barnes' story is a powerful reminder that opportunities often come disguised as humble beginnings or unexpected challenges. It's not enough to merely desire success;

one must be willing to recognise opportunities, no matter how inconspicuous they may seem. So, as we dive into the spring of possibilities, let's keep Edwin C. Barnes' story in mind and strive to develop the skill of recognising and seizing the hidden gems that lead to success.

Opportunity is said to have a sly habit of slipping in through the back door, often disguised as misfortune or temporary defeat. Only those who are prepared can recognise it and seize the moment. This may be why many people fail to identify opportunities. You must ask yourself: Are you wasting or taking these opportunities? (Story from Think and Grow Rich by Napoleon Hill)

ANOTHER STORY OF A MAN WHO RECOGNISED OPPORTUNITIES

In life, opportunities often present themselves in the most subtle and unassuming ways; therefore, it is essential to develop a keen sense of recognising them, much like the story of Les Brown, where he seized an opportunity disguised as misfortune. **As we have seen previously in the story of Barnes, opportunities often come knocking at the back door, veiled as temporary defeats or setbacks.** Those who are vigilant and prepared can recognise these opportunities for what they indeed are – stepping stones to a brighter future. It takes faith and courage to identify and take advantage of opportunities. Now, let us look at the story of Les Brown, which also drives home the fact that opportunities disguise themselves as setbacks, and it takes faith and courage to ride them.

Les Brown's journey from a city sanitation worker to a successful broadcaster, politician, and motivational speaker is a testament to the power of recognising and seizing opportunities. His story teaches us that opportunities are not always handed to us on a silver platter; sometimes, we must create them ourselves. Les didn't let initial rejection deter him from his dream of becoming a disc jockey.

Born into a challenging environment, he faced adversity from a young age. He and his twin brother were adopted by Mamie Brown, a kitchen worker and maid, shortly after their birth in a poverty-stricken neighbourhood. Placed in special education classes for the learning disabled in school and growing up in poverty, many might have seen these circumstances as insurmountable obstacles. However, Les had a dream of becoming a disc jockey. His passion for this dream was unwavering.

His pursuit of this goal took him to a local radio station, where he boldly approached the station manager and told him he wanted to be a disc jockey. The manager eyed this dishevelled young man in overalls and a straw hat and asked, "Do you have any background in broadcasting?" Les replied, "No, sir, I don't." "Well, son, I'm afraid we don't have a job for you then."

He was rejected due to his lack of background in broadcasting, but Les refused to accept defeat. On the second day, Les Brown met the manager and approached him like they had never met.

He introduced himself, saying, "How are you doing, Mr. Butterball? I am Les Brown."

The manager responded, "I know what your name is. What do you want?"

Brown continued, "I'd like to know if you have a job as a disc jockey, sir."

The manager replied, "Didn't I tell you yesterday that we had no job?"

Brown persisted, "Yes, sir, but I don't know if somebody got laid off or if somebody was fired, sir."

The manager informed him, "No one was fired or laid off. Get on out of here."

Undeterred, Brown returned the next day, acting like he was meeting the manager for the first time. He once again asked for the job. He repeated this process, returning to the station every day for a week inquiring about job openings. Eventually, he was taken on as an errand boy, and he accepted, considering it a humble start and viewing it as a foot in the door to his dreams. This is a man who recognises opportunities.

He saw an opportunity even in an errand boy role at a radio station. Initially, his duties involved fetching coffee and meals for the deejays who couldn't leave the studio. Over time, his passion earned him the trust of the disc jockeys, who entrusted him to chauffeur visiting celebrities in their Cadillacs. None of them suspected that young Les was actually without a driver's licence.

Les eagerly fulfilled all the tasks assigned to him at the station, going above and beyond. During his time with the deejays, he diligently observed and learned their intricate hand movements on the control panel. He remained in the control rooms, absorbing as much knowledge as possible until he was politely asked to vacate the premises. Then, during his late-night hours in his bedroom, he dedicated himself to practice and preparation, fully aware that an opportunity would eventually come his way.

One particular Saturday afternoon, while Les was at the station, he noticed a deejay named Rock consuming alcohol while on air. Les, being the sole presence in the building aside from Rock, recognised that this could potentially lead to trouble. He hovered nearby, pacing back and forth in front of the window of Rock's booth. As he did so, he quietly said to himself, "Drink, Rock, drink!"

Les was hungry, and he was ready. When the phone rang, Les jumped on it. It was the station manager, as he knew it would be.

"Les, this is Mr. Klein."

"Yes," said Les. "I know."

"Les, I don't think Rock can finish his program."

"Yes sir, I know."

"Would you call one of the other deejays to come in and take over?"

"Yes, sir. I sure will."

But when Les hung up the telephone, he said to himself, "Now, he must think I'm crazy."

Les did dial the telephone, but it wasn't to call in another deejay. He called his mother first and then his girlfriend. "You all go out on the front porch and turn up the radio because I'm about to come on the air!" he said.

He waited about 15 minutes before he called the general manager. "Mr. Klein, I can't find nobody," Les said. Mr. Klein then asked, "Young man, do you know how to work the controls in the studio?"

"Yes sir," replied Les.

Les darted into the booth, gently moved Rock aside and sat down at the turntable. He was ready! And he was hungry! He flipped on the microphone switch and said, "Look out! This is me LB, triple P – Les Brown, Your Platter Playing Poppa. There were none before me, and there will be none after me. Therefore, that makes me the one and only. Young and single and love to mingle. Certified, bona fide, indubitably qualified to bring you satisfaction, a whole lot of action. Look out, baby, I'm your lo-o-ove man."(10,11)

What do you think about this story? Could you see faith, courage, focus, and tenacity at play and, more importantly, the ability to take advantage of seemingly setbacks, which are, in the real sense, opportunities and stones for greatness? Would you align your minds to recognise the opportunities that come your way today and in days to come?

The subtle nature of opportunities often disguises them as challenges, and many fail to recognise them as such. As we emerge from the winter of challenges, keeping our senses sharp and our minds open to the possibilities ahead of us is essential. There are enormous opportunities ahead of you, and you got to see them.

Have you ever had that moment when you suddenly spot something in front of or around you that you haven't noticed for days, weeks or even months? It is like magic, right? Well, the truth is, it's no magic at all. It is just the fascinating quirk of our brains and has much to do with how we perceive the world around us. Our brain can filter the information that comes our way, so you may have a thing sitting in front of you all along and may not perceive it.

You see, our brains are incredible machines, but they can also be selective in what they choose to focus on. Imagine you're in a room filled with all sorts of objects, and one of them is something you've been searching for. But you don't find it right away because your brain is busy processing many other things. Our brains are wired to filter out information that doesn't seem immediately relevant to us.

Some time ago, I thought of getting a new phone. What struck me as uncanny was that as soon as I had settled on that particular phone, it seemed to appear everywhere I looked, almost as if the world had tuned into my thoughts. But let's be clear: did people rush out to buy the same phone just because I had it in mind? Absolutely not. Were those phones always there, lurking in the background, waiting for me to think about them? Yes. So, why was it that I hadn't noticed them until I had that particular phone on my mind? This is an example of how our brain works and how it filters opportunities out of our radar if we do not make an effort to shift gears towards recognising such open doors.

Much like those phones, opportunities often surround us, but we remain oblivious to them until we actively seek them out. It's as though our awareness is selectively tuned to what aligns with our current thoughts and desires. As the great teacher said, **"Seek, and you shall find"**(5) If you do not seek, you will not find- it is as simple as that. The opportunities did not come your way because you searched for them- they have always been there.

Biologically, our brains are wired to prioritise information that appears relevant to our current focus. Think of it as a mental spotlight. When contemplating that phone, my mental spotlight shone brightly on anything related to it, making me acutely aware of its presence in my environment. However, the phones had always been there; I just hadn't been tuned to them until I directed my thoughts and intentions toward that particular model.

Now, let's bring this back to seizing opportunities in life. Similar to my phone-seeking experience, **opportunities abound around us, waiting to be discovered. Yet, they often remain hidden in plain sight until we actively seek them.** Picture a budding entrepreneur who dreams of launching a business. They might be so fixated on the idea of landing a conventional job that they overlook the entrepreneurial prospects that surround them. These opportunities were always there, quietly waiting for recognition, but the entrepreneur's focus was elsewhere.

So, the takeaway here is this: the world is teeming with opportunities, but we must train ourselves to recognise them. We cannot rely solely on our default mode of perception because it tends to filter out what doesn't align with our immediate goals and beliefs. The more reason why we need to change our perspectives- your thoughts change you.

As you journey through the springtime of life, remain open-minded, cultivate curiosity, and remember that some of the most valuable opportunities may be right under your nose, patiently waiting for your attention. Just as I eventually spotted those phones when I started actively looking for them, you may uncover something remarkable when you purposefully seek out the opportunities surrounding you.

"Your big opportunity may be right where you are now." – Napoleon Hill

As we delve further into this chapter, we'll explore not only how to recognise opportunities but also how to nurture and harness them to propel ourselves forward. Just as spring prepares the earth for abundant growth, recognising and seizing opportunities during this season can prepare us for the transformations ahead. So, are you ready to open your eyes to the hidden opportunities that await you in the spring of life?

THREE FEET AWAY FROM GOLD

A common reason for failure often lies in the inability to look beyond setbacks and discern opportunities when it is just around the corner. Albert Einstein put it this way, *"In the middle of every difficulty lies opportunity."*

Here is another story. The story of R. U. Darby, a highly successful insurance salesman, illustrates how he learned to bounce back from a devastating defeat and, more importantly, faith, courage and patience as he sought success and a good life.

During the gold rush era, Darby's uncle set off for the West with the grand ambition of striking it rich. Upon arriving in Colorado, he heard tales of daily gold discoveries and wasted no time staking his claim. Armed with a pick and shovel, he toiled tirelessly, driven by his boundless energy and enthusiasm.

Weeks of gruelling labour finally bore fruit as he uncovered glimmering specks in the mud. Elation washed over him as he realised his dream of wealth was within reach. But as he contemplated the potential of his discovery, he faced a harsh reality: extracting the ore required machinery and drilling equipment. Without hesitation, he buried the mine and returned to his home in Maryland.

First, he shared the exciting news with his nephew, Rill Darby, who, in turn, enlisted the help of friends and relatives to raise funds for the necessary equipment.

With their equipment ready, Darby and his uncle returned to Colorado to resume mining. The initial ore they extracted confirmed that they had stumbled upon one of Colorado's richest veins. Encouraged by the returns, they continued to drill fervently. Then, inexplicably, the gold vein disappeared. They were left empty-handed despite their efforts to dig deeper and recover it.

Months of fruitless labour forced them to concede defeat and sell the mine and machinery. A junk dealer offered them a meagre sum, which they accepted gratefully. However, recognising the mine's potential, the dealer sought expert advice and discovered that the gold vein had yet to disappear but had merely shifted a few feet away. He resumed drilling and soon became a multi-millionaire.

Meanwhile, R. U. Darby had established a thriving insurance business. He harboured no self-pity or self-blame when he learned of the mine's newfound riches. Instead, he viewed his past failure as a valuable lesson.

He had lost a vast fortune because he had stopped drilling just three feet from gold. Had he discerned that the opportunity was just 3 feet away? He resolved to apply this lesson to his sales career, vowing never to stop at "no." He would persistently try again and again.

This insight, gleaned from his failure, propelled Darby to become one of the most successful figures in the insurance industry. History teaches us that some of the most remarkable achievements arise from the ashes of profound defeats, which shows that the springs of opportunities follow the winter. We should be keen to see them and take advantage.(12)

SUFFERING AMID OPPORTUNITY

Life is beautiful as it presents us with enormous doors of breakthroughs. The unfortunate thing is that these opportunities have a window in which they may fizzle out, and to make it worse, they do not come announcing themselves from the rooftops as chances for greatness. Instead, they often come disguised as hardship and setbacks. Albert Einstein wisely said, *'In the middle of every difficulty lies opportunity.'* Despite the many doors of greatness set before us, many fail to recognise them for various reasons. Our preconceived perceptions about life and success sometimes make us look away from these opportunities. We often desire success to be served to us on a silver platter, which is not always the case. As Helen Keller aptly stated, *"When one door of happiness closes, another opens, but often we look so long at the closed door that we do not see the one which has been opened for us."* The more reason why it was said that *"Opportunities don't happen. You create them."* by Chris Grosser.

Opportunities are not mere accidents but intricately woven threads of energy waiting for the right moment to reveal themselves. From the vantage point of quantum physics, we understand that everything in the universe is interconnected through energy. Our thoughts, emotions, and actions radiate vibrations into this vast cosmic web, shaping our reality in profound ways. When we set our intentions on a particular goal or dream, we send out energetic signals that resonate with the frequencies of our desires.

These energetic vibrations create ripples, much like dropping a stone into a calm pond. As these ripples spread, they intersect with other vibrations and circumstances in the universe. Opportunities emerge at these crossroads of energy, often appearing as discoveries by chance. It's as if the universe conspires to align people, situations, and resources in your favour, all in response to your energetic call.

This must be considered, as the energy we send out matters a lot. When we emit positive energies, the universe aligns itself to bring forth resources that amplify this positivity. Conversely, if we project negativity, the universe responds in kind. Some people refer to this phenomenon as good or bad luck, but in reality, we stand at the centre of it all; we get to decide which of the two we want to invite into our lives.

Imagine subjecting two individuals, one with a positive mindset and the other with a negative disposition, to the same challenging circumstances. They will each experience different outcomes. The positive one will ride on the wings of hardship to harness the vast resources of the universe for greatness. At the same time, the negative individual will sink deeper into misfortune, sapping energy from the universe as well. It's akin to the wisdom of the ancient saying given to the twelve spies and Israel, **"Just as you have spoken in My hearing, so I will do to you."**(13)

The catch is that these opportunities often remain hidden in plain sight, requiring us to be attuned to the subtle shifts in our surroundings. Just like a skilled surfer waits patiently for the right wave, we must learn to recognise and ride the waves of opportunity the universe sends us. This requires heightened awareness, mindfulness, and openness to the unexpected. **When we cultivate this state of**

receptivity, we become co-creators with the universe, actively shaping our destiny by harnessing the energies around us.

Thus far in this book, we have looked at some stories of people who turned their setbacks, which were opportunities, into greatness. We will not stop at that, as we will look at another fascinating story that came alive to me while I was in a gathering in college some years back.

It was at the tail end of the semester while we were taking our semester exams. It is a custom for us to gather as students to encourage one another by sharing wisdom from the Bible and praying together. It was a daily meeting that spanned the exam period. The meeting averaged forty minutes each day. These were great moments as we were energised to face the hurdles ahead.

It was a cool evening. The breeze beat gently on my skin as I hurried to find a seat among my fellow students- a concrete seat plastered to the floor, which spanned the length of the football pitch along its edge. Sometimes, it is difficult to see the end of the row as we are seated, waiting for the speaker to share his thoughts.

After a moment of music, came up this young man who gained my admiration after sharing his thoughts. He recounted the story of Hagar and how, despite her extreme thirst and being close to death, she failed to see the well right in front of her- she suffered amid plenty and opportunity.

Let's take a moment to reflect on this story and explore how possibilities can be right under our noses, yet we may suffer if we fail to recognise them.

In Beersheba's vast and unforgiving wilderness, Hagar wandered aimlessly with her young son, Ishmael. She had been sent away by Abraham, the boy's father, due to a family dispute with Sarah, Abraham's wife. Lost, and with their water supply dwindling, Hagar was overwhelmed by despair. She couldn't bear to see her child suffer, so she placed him in the shade of a bush and moved away, unable to watch his demise.

As the sun bore down mercilessly and the last drops of water were consumed, Hagar wept bitterly. It was in this moment of utter desperation that something extraordinary happened. The cries of young Ishmael reached the heavens, and God, in His mercy, heard them. An angel was sent to comfort Hagar, assuring her that God had taken notice of her plight.

"Go to him and comfort him, for I will make a great nation from his descendants,"(14) the angel declared. But there was more to this divine intervention than met the eye- God opened her eyes to a well previously unseen in her despair.

In her distress, Hagar had been blind to the life-saving water source right before her. It reminded us that **opportunities often exist in our lives, hidden in plain sight, waiting for us to recognise them.** Like Hagar, we may find ourselves in desolate situations, consumed by our troubles, and unable to see the solutions right before us.

We will continue to suffer in the face of abundance if we refuse to identify the opportunities and resources set before us. The best thing that can happen to us is to be guided to open doors or to identify opportunities, which are usually wrapped with the linen of setbacks.

Chapter Four

SEIZING THE SPRING OF OPPORTUNITIES. TAKE ADVANTAGE!

"Success is the sum of small efforts repeated day in and day out" - Robert Collier

It was a great moment going through some stories in the last chapter. Now, it is time to learn about the seven keys to recognising and taking advantage of opportunities in the spring of our lives.

SEVEN KEYS TO RECOGNISING AND TAKING ADVANTAGE OF OPPORTUNITIES

As we have seen, in life, opportunities often present themselves in the subtlest of forms, camouflaged amid the fabric of our daily challenges and experiences.

As we journey through the spring season of opportunities, we must equip ourselves with the keys to recognising these hidden potential gems.

Just as Hagar later identifies the well she had missed despite her daring needs, and Les Brown and Edwin C. Barnes, who identified that a seeming setback is opportunities disguised, we too must learn to discern the doors of opportunity that quietly await us.

Therefore, in this chapter, we will delve into the seven keys that will help us unlock the treasure chest of opportunities, empowering us to seize life's abundant possibilities. These keys are crucial for us to live a good and better life, which we deserve. Everyone deserves a great life, and the universe is filled with chances to help us achieve the kind of life we deserve. So, let us embark on this enlightening journey, uncovering the secrets to identifying the opportunities that lie before us and, most of the time, right under our noses.

Key 1: Cultivate a Positive Mindset

The first key to recognising and seizing opportunities, undoubtedly the most crucial, is **cultivating a positive mindset.** This key lays the foundation upon which all other keys rely. If you stumble at this initial step, the effectiveness of every subsequent key diminishes. I would go as far as to say that a positive mindset is the master key to unlocking the doors of opportunity in your life.

If you aspire to change your life for the better, the first transformation must occur within your mind. You don't necessarily need to alter the external circumstances that surround you; rather, the primary focus should be on changing yourself, particularly your mindset. The term "mindset" implies that the *"mind"* can be *"set"*, much like how concrete solidifies.

Consequently, changing a set mind demands a consistent and purposeful effort. It's no wonder that the wisdom of Solomon advises us to **"guard our heart with all diligence, for out of it springs the issues of life"**(15) and in another translation, it says, **"Guard your heart above all else, for it determines the course of your life."**(16) Protecting your mind and controlling what gains access to it requires diligence. Yet, it is a worthy endeavour because your life inevitably follows the direction of your thoughts- your thoughts determine the course of your life. In essence, you are your thoughts. Therefore, cultivating a positive mindset is essential to recognise and seize opportunities.

To delve deeper into this concept, it's vital to understand that a positive mindset doesn't mean denying the existence of challenges. Instead, it's about maintaining an attitude that empowers you to overcome obstacles, learn from setbacks, and see the potential for growth in every situation. It's the ability to view difficulties as opportunities in disguise.

A positive mindset is like sunshine after a rainy day; it brightens everything. It's about believing in yourself and your abilities. When you wake up, tell yourself that great opportunities await you. This mindset is a filter, helping you see the good in every situation. For example, if you face a setback at work, a positive mindset will allow you to see it as a chance to learn and grow. So, start each day with a smile, and you'll be surprised how many opportunities will come your way.

"When one door of happiness closes, another opens; but often we look so long at the closed door that we do not see the one which has been opened for us." – Helen Keller

Nine Ways to Cultivate a Positive Mindset

Cultivating a positive mindset is akin to a farmer tending to his fields. Your mind serves as the fertile soil, and reaping its benefits necessitates a process of cultivation—beginning with soil preparation, sowing seeds, tending the crop, and weeding out weeds before the harvest. Clearly, this isn't a day's job; it involves weeks and even months of dedicated effort. However, it is an endeavour that reaps rich rewards. Now, let's explore nine ways to cultivate a positive mindset.

1. **Read impactful books:** Engage with literature that has the potential to transform your life. You may be just one book away from your breakthrough. Establishing a habit of reading impactful books is of paramount importance. Your solution might be concealed within the pages of a book authored by someone who faced similar challenges in the past. Reading can save you years of trial and error. By delving into the insights and strategies these authors share, you gain the advantage of standing on the shoulders of those who have come before you.

This is undeniably one of the key ways to cultivate a positive mindset.

2. **Listen to impactful teachings:** Similar to reading books, actively engaging with impactful audio content, such as podcasts and audiobooks, among others.

   Research from Harvard University found that the average American adult spends an average of 101 minutes driving each day.(17,18) Based on Harvard's figures, the average commuter could listen to almost 50 extra books in a year since many audiobooks are under eight hours long.(17,19) Can you imagine your life if you could listen to 50 books in one year?

3. **Surround Yourself with Positive People:** Spend time with people who uplift and inspire you. The people around you rub on you and emit energies that can impact you positively or otherwise. So you want positive people around

you as this will help you cultivate positive mindsets.

4. **Set short and long-term goals:** Setting goals is a fundamental key to cultivating a positive mindset because it provides a clear sense of purpose and direction. When you set meaningful goals, you give yourself something to strive for, which can be incredibly motivating. This sense of purpose and motivation inherently fosters positivity because it shifts your focus from dwelling on problems or uncertainties to actively working toward solutions and growth.

Moreover, setting goals helps you envision a better future, a cornerstone of a positive mindset. By defining what you want to achieve, you paint a mental picture of success, and this visualisation can serve as a powerful source of inspiration and optimism. As you progress toward your goals, even small steps forward can boost your confidence and reinforce the belief that you have control over your destiny. It's not just about reaching the end goal but also about the journey and personal growth that occurs along the way, which can significantly contribute to a positive and empowered mindset. In essence, setting and pursuing goals not only provide structure to your life but also infuse it with a sense of purpose and optimism.

5. **Practice Gratitude:** Regularly expressing appreciation for the good things in your life, no matter how small they may seem, helps you put on a positive mindset even when things are not going how you want.

6. **Embrace Failure:** One of the essential keys to cultivating a positive mindset is to embrace failure as a natural part of the journey toward success. The journey to success is not a straight line; it is curvy with mountains and valleys and, of course, pastures along the way.

Failures are not setbacks but stepping stones to growth and resilience. As the legendary basketball player Michael Jordan once said, ***"I've missed more than 9,000 shots in my career. I've lost almost 300 games. Twenty-six times, I've been trusted to take the game-winning shot and missed. I've failed over and over and over again in my life. And that is why I succeed."***

Embracing failure means learning from mistakes, adapting, and persisting despite setbacks. It recognises that every stumble brings you closer to your goals, as Winston Churchill noted: ***"Success is not final, failure is not fatal: It is the courage to continue that counts."*** When you view failure as a valuable teacher rather than an adversary, you nurture a positive mindset that thrives on resilience, perseverance, and the unwavering belief that setbacks are inscribed into the path to success.

It is good to know that failure is part of winning and not the opposite of winning.

7. **Embrace the Present. Let Go of the Past:** Another essential key to cultivating a positive mindset is to free yourself from the shackles of the past. Dwelling on past mistakes, regrets, or missed opportunities can weigh heavily on your psyche and hinder your ability to seize new opportunities in the present. As Eckhart Tolle wisely noted, ***"Realise deeply that the present moment is all you ever have."*** Embracing the present moment allows you to fully engage with your current circumstances and possibilities, unburdened by the baggage of the past.

8. **Limit Exposure to Negativity:** Another crucial key to cultivating a positive mindset is limiting exposure to negativity, which includes reducing consumption of negative news, media, and influences that bring you down. In a world of

constant information, it's essential to filter out sources that perpetuate negativity and focus on what uplifts and inspires. Remember, you can curate your media intake, ensuring it aligns with your goals and values. Doing so creates a mental environment conducive to nurturing positivity, enabling you to seize the spring of opportunities with a renewed sense of optimism.

9. **Celebrate Small Wins:** Acknowledge and celebrate your achievements, no matter how minor they may seem, as it is also pivotal to cultivating a positive mindset. Rejoicing in the little victories along the way matters.

As Mark Twain stated, ***"The secret of getting ahead is getting started."*** No matter how small, each step propels you forward and validates your efforts. By acknowledging and appreciating these incremental achievements, you boost your self-esteem and have a cheerful disposition to life even if you have not gotten what you wanted. Remember that accumulating these small victories gives room to the so-called big success. As Robert Collier wisely said, *"Success is the sum of small efforts repeated day in and day out."* So, in the pursuit of seizing the spring of opportunities, remember that the small wins ultimately lead to grand triumphs.

Key 2: Keep Learning

We've discussed the first key to recognising and seizing opportunities. I trust you've learned from it and are eager to apply this key to unlock the treasures of opportunities that surround you. Now, let's embark on our journey into the second key, equally vital in capitalising on the Spring of Opportunities: **Keep Learning.** This key is crucial on the path to seizing opportunities.

One of the defining characteristics of successful individuals is their unwavering commitment to continuous learning. They continue to expand their wealth of knowledge and refine their skills, upskill or re-skill. As illustrated in the story of Les Brown, who aspired to be a DJ but found himself working as an errand boy at a radio station- successful people utilise every opportunity to learn and grow. While performing his duties as an errand boy, Les Brown keenly observed and absorbed the DJ's artistry in the studio. This proactive approach positioned him for a forthcoming opportunity when he was asked to fill in for a DJ who had overindulged in drinks- he was hungry and prepared for the position. Seneca, the Roman Philosopher, aptly expressed this concept with his famous words, ***"Luck is what happens when preparation meets opportunity."*** If you aspire to be fortunate, you must continue learning, regardless of your current inclination. Remember that success is doing what you need to do when you need to, whether you feel like it or not. So you do not have to feel like learning before you learn because usually, you will not feel like it. If you wait until you feel like learning before you do, you may not learn anything new.

Have you ever considered how much more comfortable it is for us to spend time watching movies or playing rather than working or acquiring new knowledge? Often, we may not even pay attention to the amount of time devoted to entertainment, and it doesn't require any special preparation to indulge in these pleasures. In contrast, when it comes to learning, it demands a conscious effort to keep ourselves engaged and disciplined enough to develop a habit of continuous learning. However, as you persevere in this journey, you will find that continuing to learn gradually becomes a habit, making it easier to engage in learning without giving it a second thought.

The beauty of learning is that age is no barrier; you can never be too old to learn. By embracing a mindset of continuous learning, you position yourself to reap the bountiful rewards of the spring season of life. So, keep learning, and you'll undoubtedly tap into the abundance that awaits.

Key 3: Be Curious

As we explore the keys to recognising and seizing opportunities, we come to another key that can transform your life and open doors to uncharted territories and possibilities: **"Be Curious."** This key harmonises beautifully with the preceding ones, as cultivating a positive mindset and continually learning are like the fertile soil that births and nurtures the growth of curiosity.

Imagine a world where people were content with the status quo, where the spirit of exploration lay dormant, and where questions were seldom asked. Such a world would be devoid of innovation, progress, and the countless breakthroughs that have shaped our lives. Thankfully, we live in a world where curiosity has sparked the most incredible discoveries, from the invention of electricity to the exploration of space.

Curiosity is the compass that guides us through the uncharted territories of opportunities. It propels us to ask questions, seek new experiences, and embrace the unknown. It is the driving force behind great inventions, scientific breakthroughs, and entrepreneurial success stories.

The Seven Spiritual Laws of Success, written by Deepak Chopra, begin with the Law of Pure Potentiality. This law reveals our immense capabilities, often hidden from the naked eye. Our vast potential requires a certain level of curiosity to unearth. This is likewise important to transform the unmanifest into the manifest. To harness various opportunities, we must nurture our sense of curiosity.

It's worth noting that everything we observe initially exists in the unseen realm, and it takes curious minds to explore the intangible and make it tangible in the physical world. As Pierre Teilhard de Chardin, the French philosopher, wisely stated, *'We are not human beings having a spiritual experience. We are spiritual beings having a human experience.'* This reminds us not to settle for what our physical senses perceive alone. Instead, we must nurture our curiosity to tap into our spiritual experiences, a vital step in preventing opportunities from slipping through our grasp.

Think of the story of Thomas Edison, the man who gave us the electric light bulb. Edison's relentless curiosity led him to conduct hundreds of experiments in his quest to find a suitable filament for the light bulb. When asked about his failures, he famously replied, *"I have not failed. I've just found 10,000 ways that won't work."* His curiosity was insatiable, ultimately leading to one of the most transformative inventions in history.

Similarly, your curiosity can lead you to opportunities that others overlook. When you approach life with a curious spirit, you are more likely to spot the hidden doors of opportunity that others walk past without a second glance. You become an explorer of the unknown, a seeker of hidden treasures, and a pioneer of new paths.

So, as you journey through the spring of opportunities, remember to cultivate a curious mindset. Embrace each day as an opportunity to learn, explore, and discover. Ask questions, seek answers, and never stop wondering about the wonders ahead. With curiosity as your guide, you'll be well-prepared to recognise and seize the abundant opportunities that await you on this remarkable journey. As said by the great teacher, Jesus Christ, **"Seek and you shall find."**(5) **Be Curious!**

Key 4: Build Networks

As we delve deeper into the keys for recognising and seizing opportunities during the vibrant spring season in a man's life, our journey brings us to this pivotal key: **"Build Networks."** This key doesn't exist in isolation but is interconnected with the previous ones – cultivating a positive mindset, continually learning, and nurturing curiosity. Just as spring breathes life into the world, your network can breathe life into your opportunities.

Imagine the world as a vast garden and each person you meet as a unique flower. Every connection you make adds a new hue, fragrance, or texture to this ever-expanding garden. Your network is not just about the number of people you know but the depth and diversity of those connections. It's not merely a list of contacts in your phone but a living, breathing ecosystem of relationships.

The power of your network lies in its ability to expose you to new perspectives, ideas, and opportunities. It's a treasure trove of knowledge and experiences waiting to be tapped into. When you surround yourself with people from various backgrounds, industries, and walks of life, you create a dynamic environment where opportunities can flourish.

In one of Robert Kiyosaki's books, he emphasised that it is not about what you can do but who you know that can do it. This underscores the importance of building viable and impactful networks of people.

Your network can be a source of mentorship, guidance, and support. It can connect you with the right people who can open doors to opportunities you might not have found on your own. Your network can be your launchpad for reaching new heights.

This is a story that illustrates the importance of building the right networks. Peter, Jesus' disciple, was known for his outspoken and daring nature, yet when his master was brought into the high priest's residence, he found himself unable to gain entry. He lacked the necessary network of connections to secure access. In contrast, another disciple with a relationship with the high priest went unhindered. Later, this same disciple intervened on Peter's behalf and spoke to the gatekeeper, facilitating Peter's entry. Had Peter not established a network with the disciple who was known by the high priest, he might have remained outside the courtyard throughout the night. This narrative underscores the importance of building and nurturing networks.

Reference to the story: 'And Simon Peter followed Jesus, and so did another disciple. Now that disciple was known to the high priest and went with Jesus into the courtyard of the high priest. But Peter stood at the door outside. Then the other disciple, who was known to the high priest, went out and spoke to her who kept the door and brought Peter in.' (John 18:15, 16)

In the spring of opportunities, building and nurturing your network is akin to planting seeds in fertile soil. As you connect with others, you're sowing the seeds of possibility. Just as spring showers water the earth, your efforts in building relationships can lead to a bountiful harvest of opportunities. So, build networks.

Key 5: Setting Clear Goals

We are not finished with our voyage of discovering the keys to identifying and seizing the often abundant opportunities that surround us. Building upon the foundation of cultivating a positive mindset, continuous learning, nurturing curiosity, and expanding your network, we now embark on our next essential key: **"Setting Clear Goals."** This key can not be overemphasised, for without it, we risk drifting aimlessly on the sea of life, easily distracted by the myriads of pseudo-opportunities surrounding us. Having clear goals serves as our compass, allowing us to navigate the vast sea of possibilities and select those that align with our purpose and life's goals.

You need clarity of purpose to discern between the good and the right. Purpose keeps you focused on the right things and guards you from being distracted by the good.

Imagine your goals as guiding stars in the vast night sky of opportunities. Just as sailors once relied on the North Star to navigate the uncharted seas, setting clear goals serves as your compass in the ocean of possibilities. It's your roadmap to ensure you don't drift aimlessly but stay on course towards your desired destination.

Opportunities often ambiguously present themselves. Without clear goals, you might not spot an opportunity and may lack the ability to harness it effectively. Setting clear goals acts as a beacon, helping you recognise opportunities that align with your aspirations. When you know where you're heading, you can readily identify the paths that will lead you there.

Edwin had an unambiguous goal: to become Thomas Edison's partner. This clear objective guided his route with a keen insight into recognising the open doors leading to the man he aspired to partner with. Even when offered a job far from his aspiration, that of a sweeper, he didn't waver due to his unwavering sense of purpose. Having such a clear goal in life helps you identify the resources in front of you and paves the way for achieving remarkable success.

The same principle applies to Les Brown, as we've seen earlier. His clear sense of purpose and goals fueled his persistence, even after facing multiple rejections. When offered the role of an errand boy, he viewed it as a stepping stone toward his dreams. It's incredibly challenging to deter individuals who are resolute in their purpose and life goals. This conviction ignites an unquenchable thirst and passion, enabling them to spot opportunities that others, without clear life goals, might overlook while drifting aimlessly through life without a destination.

As Martin Luther King Jr. articulated, *'A man who has not found something he is willing to die for is not fit to live.'* This underscores the importance of having a clear goal and purpose in life, as it gives an individual a reason to live. When one possesses a clear life goal, one not only finds meaning but also develops a hunger for opportunities. Such individuals are bound to uncover the opportunities that surround them.

Your goals act as filters, allowing you to sift through life's myriad opportunities. They enable you to discern which options align with your vision and which may lead you astray. When you have clear goals, you can quickly assess whether a particular opportunity moves you closer to your dreams or distracts you from your path.

I authored a book that delves into the art of setting clear goals, a crucial aspect of achieving significant success. I invite you to explore the book's pages if you seek further insights. The book is titled '**From Overwhelmed to Organized: A Time Management Blueprint for Busy Professionals.**' [https://www.amazon.co.uk/dp/B0BSVHBLFV]

Key 6: Self Discipline

Thus far, we've learnt the importance of cultivating a positive mindset, the value of continuous learning, the curiosity that fuels discovery, the power of building a solid network, and the necessity of setting clear goals. As we delve deeper into the keys to identifying and seizing opportunities, we arrive at the sixth key, which is no other but **"self-discipline"**.

Self-discipline is the bridge that connects aspiration with achievement. Without self-discipline, our dreams and aspirations will remain in the intangible world. It takes discipline to transform the intangible into what we can see and benefit from. The world will only benefit from your gifts and potential if you embrace self-discipline. Self-discipline is the compass that keeps us on course when distraction and temptation threaten to lead us astray from our destinations.

Self-discipline is also the invaluable ability to control and regulate one's actions, thoughts, and behaviours to pursue a specific goal or desired outcome. It involves the conscious choice to prioritise long-term objectives over immediate gratification or distractions.

Self-disciplined individuals are long-term thinkers. They exhibit resilience in the face of challenges and consistently focus on their goals and visions, even when faced with temptations or obstacles. As Aristotle wisely noted, *"We are what we repeatedly do. Excellence, then, is not an act, but a habit."*

Brian Tracy noted in one of his books that everything starts hard before becoming easy. This is where self-discipline comes into play. You need self-discipline to cultivate the commitment and preparation required for the opportunities that will be presented to you.

Distraction is the arch-enemy of self-discipline and a hindrance to achieving success and one's full potential. I wrote extensively on ways to eliminate distractions in one of my books, **'From Overwhelmed to Organised: A Time Management Blueprint for Busy Professionals.'** You can get the book [https://www.amazon.co.uk/dp/B0BSVHBLFV].

Among the strategies to avoid distractions, I found a tool particularly effective in eliminating distractions. You may be wondering what this tool is and how to engage it. I will share this all-time effective tool and how to effectively engage it soon. Before I mention the tool, let's lay the foundation to understand the tool better. So, let's get started!

Discipline is training your mind and actions to follow a set of rules or a specific course of action. It involves developing good habits, setting boundaries, and adhering to standards or expectations. This is especially important to stay on track and to achieve a set goal. The antidote to distraction is discipline: being able to do what you should do at the right time and place. If you are not unnecessarily distracted, then you are disciplined. It takes discipline to stay on track, as there will always be things that will compete for your attention.

There is more to discipline than the above, as the force behind it can be within or without. This leads us to the subject of self-discipline. When the force behind keeping you on track to success is within, it is called self-discipline. Self-discipline is the ability to control your thoughts, actions, and behaviours all by yourself. It involves setting goals and working towards them without being pushed by anyone, even when you don't feel like it or when distractions surround you. Self-discipline is often considered a key component of success and can be especially important for you as you seek success.

One striking difference between discipline and self-discipline is that discipline is often imposed from the outside, while self-discipline is self-motivated. For example, discipline might be imposed by a teacher, parent, or boss, while self-discipline comes from within.

Additionally, discipline tends to focus on following rules or standards, while self-discipline focuses more on personal growth and achievement.

Another difference between discipline and self-discipline is that discipline tends to be more reactive, while self-discipline is proactive. Discipline is often used to correct or prevent negative behaviours, while self-discipline is proactively working towards a specific goal or objective and avoiding negative behaviours that will deter the individual from achieving the goals.

Again, discipline and self-discipline can have different effects on your overall well-being. Discipline may be seen as a form of punishment or control, which can lead to feelings of resentment or frustration. Self-discipline, however, can lead to a sense of accomplishment, self-esteem and personal growth, helping you feel more fulfilled and satisfied with your life.

There are various tools like web blockers, time-tracking apps and devices with "do not disturb" features that can help eliminate distractions. However, I have found that one tool stands above the rest when it comes to eliminating distractions and is thus the greatest of all: self-discipline fueled by a passion for a lifetime vision or goal.

Self-discipline is the most powerful discipline on earth, and there is no greater self-discipline than one driven by a passion or inner strength to achieve a lifetime goal or vision. When you are convinced and passionate about a lifetime vision, you will be self-disciplined and able to overcome distractions. This is the most incredible tool of all. Prayer and fasting can't do what this tool can. The answer to your prayers and fasting for overcoming distractions is insight and passion for a lifetime goal and vision. Without self-discipline fueled by a passion for a purpose, every other tool to eliminate distractions will fail.

No motivational force can be compared to the energy or passion for achieving a lifetime goal or vision. Nothing can quench such motivation as long as the individual is convinced of the vision.

Conviction about a lifetime or short-term goal is more than just discussing it. It is an inner energy and belief in the vision. Anyone who gets to this point can discipline themselves to align appropriately to achieve the vision.

Passion is a strong and intense emotion or enthusiasm for something. It's a feeling that drives you to pursue your interests with energy and dedication. Passion is a powerful source of motivation, helping you stay focused and committed to your goals. The energy derived from passion can break boundaries and go through any problematic situation. A passionate man cannot be discouraged because their source of courage is within and not from their outer environment. The only thing that can stop a passionate man is discouragement from within. As long as they do not lose sight of what they have seen about themselves that others have not seen, they cannot be discouraged. Interestingly, what is supposed to be a discouragement fuels them to action and gives them more energy as they see it as a motivation toward their goals.

History is full of passionate men who tread the paths of difficulty and discouragement in strength and courage because they are convinced of their life vision and goals. One thing is familiar to them: they are self-disciplined. They need no one to tell them what they are supposed to do because their motivation is from within. While no one watches, they get to work and are not easily distracted.

Passion can fuel self-discipline by providing a solid sense of purpose or meaning. When you're passionate about something, you're more likely to be motivated to work towards the goals, even when it's not easy. Additionally, passion can help you stay focused and avoid getting sidetracked by distractions, as you're more likely to be engaged and invested in your work. Passionate individuals do not have the time for gossip, unnecessary chats and other distractions since their goals are usually bigger than them, and they are pressed to make every minute count to achieve the goals. They work as though more than the time allocated to them is needed to achieve their objectives; thus, they are buried in their work and are not easily sidetracked. So, if you are distracted and have tried several strategies with no success, here is the ultimate solution: self-discipline fuelled by a passion for a lifetime vision. Every other thing falls in place when you get this right.

Consider the story of Thomas Edison, a man whose self-discipline and perseverance were instrumental in seizing opportunities that transformed the world. He famously said, ***"Genius is one per cent inspiration and ninety-nine per cent perspiration."*** His relentless pursuit of innovation, fueled by an unwavering commitment to his goals, led to the invention of the electric light bulb and other breakthroughs. Edison's self-discipline allowed him to see opportunities where others saw only obstacles.

I welcome you to your world of opportunities and success as you harness this invaluable key called Self-Discipline.

Key 7: Stay Persistent and Consistent

Undoubtedly, you have been equipped with enough keys to identify and take advantage of the opportunities around you. Before we bring this subject to a close, let us look at the seventh key: **"Stay Persistent and Consistent"**.

Persistence is the unwavering commitment to a goal or vision, even when the road is laden with challenges and setbacks. As you journey through life, it won't always unfold as expected, but persistence will help you stay on course regardless of the situation. It is the driving force that enables you to remain steadfast, even in the face of inevitable trials. This quality can transform curiosity into innovation, goals into accomplishments, and dreams into reality.

Consider the story of J.K. Rowling. Before her "Harry Potter" series became a global phenomenon, Rowling faced rejection after rejection from publishers. Her manuscript was submitted to twelve publishers, all of which rejected it.(20) But she persisted, holding fast to her dream of sharing the magical world she had created. Her resilience paid off, leading to one of history's most successful book franchises. Her persistence brought her dream to life.

In life, staying persistent is vital to success. **Understand that challenges are not roadblocks but stepping stones to success.** Remember that **persistence turns adversity into growth and setbacks into comebacks.** As you continue your journey to seize the spring of opportunities, keep the flame of persistence burning brightly within you, for it is the beacon that guides you toward the remarkable achievements that await in this season of your life.

You are more able than you can ever imagine!

Chapter Five

THE SEED TIME!

"Act like people with good sense and not like fools. These are evil times, so make every minute count. Don't be stupid. Instead, find out what the Lord wants you to do. Don't destroy yourself by getting drunk, but let the Spirit fill your life." - Eph 5:15-18 CEV

"So watch your step. Use your head. Make the most of every chance you get. These are desperate times! Don't live carelessly, unthinkingly. Make sure you understand what the Master wants." - Eph 5:15-17 THE MESSAGE

We once lived in a different part of the country before moving to the southwestern part. When I arrived there as a young boy, I had the chance to meet several people, primarily farmers. I joined them on the farm and relished the gentle breeze and the unique, delicious food on the farm. It had a distinctive taste and was incredibly sumptuous. What more could I have asked for? I thoroughly enjoyed this aspect of my experience on the farm.

One day, out of curiosity, I asked why they couldn't plant certain crops at any time of the year. They seemed to wait for a specific time, diligently preparing the soil and seeds while awaiting that moment. When the time finally came, as if chased by an invisible force, they all hurried to the fields to plant their seeds. This period was no laughing matter to them.

I received a response to my question explaining that you can't simply plant any time of the year. If you sow out of season, you won't get the desired harvest. The seeds might not even sprout, and if they do, they're likely not to bear fruit. However, by waiting patiently for this opportune planting window, they ensured the seeds they had prepared beforehand would yield the desired results.

In this book, 'Leveraging the Power of Seasons: Understanding and Taking Advantage of the Four Seasons of Life', it is time to venture into the next chapter: The Seed Time. Think of this chapter as a time to plant your seeds as you journey through life. Like the farmers above, you cannot joke with this season because it doesn't last forever.

In the previous chapters of this book, we explored how to navigate and handle the winter of challenges and how to take advantage of the spring of opportunities using the seven time-tested keys to recognise and seize possibilities. Now, let's take our journey a step further by delving into the concept of the **'Seed Time.'**

The season of spring, often referred to as a time of opportunity, is also named 'The Seed Time.' It's not merely a label; it carries a profound message about what's expected of us during this season of opportunity – to sow seeds.

This season isn't a time for idleness but a time for sowing. It's not a season for reaping; it's a season for planting seeds. As the wise Preacher proclaimed, 'For everything, there is a season, a time for every activity under heaven. A time to be born and a time to die. **A time to plant and a time to harvest.**'(21) Our lives have seasons, each with its designated purpose and time frame.

EMBRACING THE TRANSIENCE OF THE SPRING OF OPPORTUNITIES AND SEED TIME

As we dive further into this chapter, we must recognise that nothing in life, not even spring, lasts forever. The Spring of opportunities and Seed Time is likewise temporary, just as we established before now that the winter of challenges does not last forever. Spring is the season of rejuvenation, a time when nature awakens from its slumber, and opportunities bloom like colourful flowers in a garden. Yet, as nature moves through its cycles, so do our lives. The spring of opportunities is transient, and the window for planting seeds is limited. Therefore, we are supposed to take advantage of this season if we want a good harvest and success. Do not waste your seasons of opportunities because they are not infinite.

Consider, for a moment, how the cherry blossoms for a bit of time. Their brief, breathtaking display of beauty reminds us that even the most splendid moments in life are fleeting. The cherries burst forth, gracing us with their delicate pink and white petals, and then, in what seems like an instant, they drift away, leaving behind only a memory. This is the nature of seasons, and this is the nature of life.

In our journey through the seasons of life, we must learn to embrace the transience of springs. Opportunities, like the cherry, have their moments of brilliance. They arrive, sometimes unexpectedly, and present themselves for a brief period. If we fail to recognise and seize them during this fleeting window, they may disappear, much like the example of the cherry, which once blossoms and is nowhere to be found in a moment.

The lesson here is clear: the spring of opportunities, much like the seed time, is a finite period in our lives. To leverage this season's power, we must acknowledge its temporary nature and act decisively when the opportunities present themselves. Just as the cherry blossoms grace us with their beauty for a short time, opportunities grace us with the potential for growth and success. Let's make the most of it.

Imagine for a moment that you are a farmer, and you've toiled tirelessly in the spring, carefully planting seeds and nurturing your crops. The fields yield bountiful harvests as the sun and rain smile upon your efforts. The storehouses are full, and the fruits of your labour are abundant. Now, imagine for a moment if you had not planted. What would you have harvested even if the sun and rain had come to bless your works?

Weeds and thorns because the soil cannot remain empty.

Joseph's story in ancient Egypt is a profound lesson in seizing the bounty before the famine. With his gift of interpreting dreams, Joseph foresaw a time of plenty followed by a devastating famine. Recognising the transient nature of the season, he advised Pharaoh to take full advantage of the abundance. In doing so, they stored grain during the years of plenty, ensuring the survival of their people during the harsh years that followed. They embraced the transience of the season of opportunities, which you should embrace too.

Joseph's wisdom and foresight highlight the critical principle that **what we do during the seasons of opportunity profoundly impacts our ability to weather the storms of life.** In our modern context, these seasons of opportunity can be likened to periods of career growth, financial stability, or personal development. During these times, we have the chance to make choices that can safeguard our future.

Consider, for instance, the imaginary story of a young professional named Robert. Early in his career, he found himself in a thriving industry, surrounded by mentors and opportunities. He could have coasted through these years, enjoying life without considering life's inevitable changes. Instead, he chose to maintain a positive mindset, invest in continuous learning, build a robust professional network, and save and invest prudently. Remember that these are some of the seven keys to recognising and seizing opportunities we explored in the previous chapter.

Many of his colleagues struggled to adapt when the industry faced a downturn years later. However, Robert's choices during the season of plenty allowed him to weather the storm. He seamlessly transitioned into a different field and continued to thrive, showing us that seizing opportunities in spring can fortify us from the winters of life.

This story is not new, and it is not just imaginary, as there is nothing new under the sun. We have witnessed revolutions and changes in industries that have cost people their jobs and means of livelihood. Some individuals were hit so hard that they could not recover; for others, the hit presented an opportunity. The distinguishing factor lay in their preparedness during the seed time and their acceptance of the fact that nothing is permanent, be it good or otherwise. Therefore, when you have plenty, remember to plant. Take the seed time seriously. Seize every opportunity that comes your way. Think ahead and act wisely.

So, as we navigate the spring of opportunities and seed time, let us be mindful of the importance of making wise choices, just as Joseph did in Egypt. When abundance graces our lives, let us not squander it but invest in our growth, resilience, and preparedness for the seasons to come. By doing so, we ensure that we'll not only survive but thrive when the winds of change blow our way.

Remember the words of Publilius Syrus, who said, ***"The opportunity is often lost by deliberating"***. It is not time to deliberate but to work and plant your seeds.

MAKE THE MOST OF EVERY OPPORTUNITY.

There's a saying that goes, *"Carpe Diem,"* a phrase that originated from the Roman poet Horace, which translates to "Seize the Day." Some may interpret this saying as advocating for enjoying the present and disregarding the future. However, such a perspective may not always be the most prudent as it is paramount to think long-term.

Long-term thinkers are more likely to succeed than short-term thinkers because they are driven by visions of what they have seen with their minds, even if they haven't physically touched it. Like short-term thinkers, long-term thinkers may not necessarily love what they do. But unlike short-term thinkers, they still engage in these activities because they are motivated by their long-term goals.

Waking up early is a universal challenge. Everyone craves an extra hour of sleep, and the temptation to hit the snooze button is strong. However, some individuals choose to sacrifice a few hours of sleep to work because they prioritise long-term gratification over short-term pleasures. They exercise discipline, making every minute count to pursue what others merely dream about. **While everyone may have dreams and fantasies, only a selected few turn those dreams into reality. The difference lies in self-discipline and long-term thinking.**

You should embrace long-term thinking and commit to the necessary work required. While it may not be easy initially, it will get easier with time. As Brian Tracy reiterated in one of his books, **"Everything starts hard before becoming easy."** The journey may be challenging at the outset, but with more patience and consistency, you can transform it into a habit, making it as effortless as a piece of cake.

Often, we pray for deliverance from the perceived evil of the day without realising that embedded within the very fabric of that day are countless chances for us to shape our destiny. It's akin to sowing seeds in a vast field. If we squander these opportunities, we risk reaping a harvest of regret.

Years ago, I prayed to redeem the day of its evil as we were told it was full of evil. **"Redeeming the time, because the days are evil." Eph 5:16 KJV.** I prayed for deliverance from these evils for myself and my loved ones as I could not imagine anything in the day but evil until I got clarity about this verse when I came across the same verse in other translations.

One of the translations reads, '**Make the most of every opportunity in these evil days.' (NLT)** This suggests that if you wish to redeem the evil days, you must maximise every opportunity. As we've discussed earlier, seed time is the season to plant your seeds, work diligently, and make the most of every opportunity that comes your way. When you squander opportunities, you fail to redeem the evil days.

This portion of the Bible goes on to emphasise that one should not be thoughtless but should understand the will of the Lord. This means we should have a clear direction or purpose for our lives, as we explored in the previous chapter on recognising and seizing opportunities, where having clear goals was a key factor. Therefore, you cannot afford to be ignorant of the purpose of your existence. View every minute as an opportunity to sow good seeds, and you will find fulfilment along the way.

This passage revealed a profound truth—making the most of every opportunity is the key to overcoming life's challenges. Just as a farmer tends to his fields diligently, we should cultivate our lives with purpose and intent. In doing so, we not only redeem the days we perceive as evil but also transform them into stepping stones towards a brighter future. We should realise that embedded within the very fabric of each day are countless chances for us to shape our destiny.

Imagine two individuals given the same twenty-four hours in a day. One uses their time wisely, seizing every opportunity for personal growth, continuous learning, cultivating a positive mindset and embracing personal and professional progress. The other let the hours slip away, filled with distractions and procrastination. As Victor Kiam once wisely remarked, ***"Procrastination is opportunity's assassin."*** Over time, the difference between these two paths becomes apparent. The former experiences growth and success, while the latter remains stagnant, poor and maybe sick.

It is time to take responsibility for yourself. Stop blaming anyone for your life because you are the driver and the one **who determines what your life is and will be through the minor and major decisions you make each day.** Will you decide to make every minute of your life count starting from this moment?

The lesson here is crystal clear: every minute, every encounter, and every circumstance is an opportunity to plant the seeds of your dreams. **It's not enough to wish for a brighter future; you must actively cultivate it.** Just like the English proverb reiterates, *"If wishes were horses, beggars would ride."* Just as a farmer toils in the fields to reap a bountiful harvest, you must work diligently to make the most of every opportunity that comes your way.

You can revisit the previous chapter of this book to explore the keys to recognising and maximising these opportunities to ensure that you become the architect of your destiny. Remember, the universe presents us with abundant chances; it's up to us to seize them and shape our story and life.

DO NOT WASTE YOUR SEED TIME.

Imagine a farmer diligently preparing the soil, choosing the finest seeds, and then simply storing them away, never to be planted. What a waste it would be! In our own lives, we are each endowed with a unique spring—a season of opportunities, new beginnings, and the chance to sow the seeds for our dreams. Yet, many of us squander this precious time, allowing opportunities to slip through our fingers like sand.

Many refuse to act on their dreams; a dream without action is just an illusion. Successful individuals dream, take action, and then live their dreams. In reality, work comes before success; only in the dictionary does success come before work.

Some may get distracted along the way, and that's all the more reason why you need a system to keep you focused. This generation faces numerous distractions with the barrage of gadgets we have, and I think we are the most distracted.

A friend humorously shared his school experience when he asked his parents for a laptop to aid his studies. They granted his request, but he saw movies more than he studied when given the computer. The gadget that was intended to enhance his education became a significant distraction. Fast forward to the present, he mentioned how the same laptop has been a valuable tool in his profession, helping him meet targets and achieve professional growth. Like a beam of light, you must stay focused on your goals to succeed. Distractions and success do not go hand in hand.

It's also important to note that many people procrastinate when it comes to pursuing their aspirations. They waste time in fear of when and how to start. Let me be candid—there will never be a perfect time to commence working on your goals and visions. You'll wait indefinitely if you're seeking the ideal moment to launch. While you delay, time does not wait for you. As Benjamin Franklin aptly said, 'You may delay, but time will not.' Will you delay further and squander your seed time, or will you step out with courage and faith?

One of the primary reasons we procrastinate in pursuing our dreams is fear. ***Every one of us experiences fear, but what we choose to do about our fears makes the difference.*** If you claim to have never felt fear or that you cannot be afraid, you're not being truthful. Courage is not the absence of fear but the decision to act despite it. When you step out in faith, even when you are afraid, you'll discover that the fear was just an illusion all along. How many of the things we feared happened? The universe has been waiting for you to launch out all along. As the famous saying goes, ***'If you can think it, you can do it.'*** When an idea crosses your mind, it's a message from God telling you, 'You can do it'. Even if you're afraid, take that step in faith and courage, and you'll be astonished by the abundance of resources available to you.

As we journey in life, we must recognise that the seed time doesn't last forever. Just as spring transitions into summer, the season of opportunity may transform into seasons of challenge and adversity. When we neglect to seize the opportunities presented during our spring, we squander our limited seed time, which we should not allow. As the saying goes, *"Opportunity knocks but once."* Each moment, each encounter, and each opportunity is like a seed waiting to be planted. Yet, it's up to us to recognise these moments, till the soil of our lives, and sow our aspirations, for they are the seeds for our future.

One key lesson from the story of Joseph in Egypt illustrates the importance of using our seed time effectively. Joseph foresaw seven years of plenty, followed by seven years of famine. This knowledge of the transience of the time of plenty helped him to advise that a portion of their produce be stored in preparation for the harsh season in the future. Joseph recognised the transient nature of opportunities and took full advantage of the time of plenty to ensure survival during the challenging times ahead. His wisdom echoes through the ages as a reminder that we must embrace opportunities fully when they arise, as they may not return in the same abundance.

As I conclude this section, here is the reminder: **"Do not waste your Seed Time!"**

LEARNING FROM THE ANT

The ants stand out among creatures who understand the time and seasons. These industrious creatures teach us invaluable lessons about seizing the right moments and making the most of each season. While their small size might lead us to underestimate their wisdom, the ants are, in fact, diligent planners, master workers, and superb organisers. Their actions are a testament to the profound intelligence ingrained in the natural world. As affirmed by King Solomon, **"The ants are a people not strong, Yet they prepare their food in the summer."**(22)

Ants epitomise the essence of understanding the seasons. The ants undergo distinct seasonal cycles as humans experience different phases and opportunities. During the spring and summer, these tiny but mighty creatures hustle tirelessly, collecting food with unwavering determination. They understand the essence of planting and gathering during the right season, ensuring their reserves are filled.

This is a profound lesson for us. In our own lives, we often let precious opportunities slip through our fingers simply because we fail to recognise the season we are in. The ant's diligence reminds us that there is a time for everything under the sun—a time to work, a time to save and invest, and a time to rest. Just as the ant gathers provisions during the spring and summer, we should seize our moments of opportunity. When the sun shines brightly on our paths, we should plant the seeds of our dreams, work diligently, and prepare for the seasons of challenges that are sure to come.

The ant's unwavering commitment to its tasks teaches us the power of self-motivation and initiative. Without a queen ant directing their every move, individual ants instinctively know their roles and take the initiative to perform them. This level of self-organisation and self-motivation is a testament to their incredible work ethic and ability to function as a harmonious community. It serves as a reminder that, in our own lives, we should not wait for external forces to guide us. Instead, we should possess the inner fire and determination to seize opportunities, organise our actions, and work diligently toward our goals.

As we delve deeper into the lessons from the ant, we realise that they are not merely efficient but also excellent planners. Ants do not randomly scatter their efforts; they have a strategic approach to their work. They prioritise their tasks based on the season and the colony's needs. This meticulous planning ensures that they make the most of their opportunities. It illustrates how we, too, should approach our lives—strategically, with a clear understanding of our seasons and a well-thought-out plan for our pursuits.

In conclusion, the ant, though small in size, teaches us profound lessons about understanding the seasons of life. Their unwavering commitment to their work, their initiative, their excellent planning, and their remarkable teamwork serve as inspirations for us. We should strive to recognise the seasons we are in, make the most of our opportunities, and work diligently, with a sense of purpose, to achieve our goals. As the saying goes, **"Go to the ant, O sluggard; consider her ways, and be wise."**(23)

THE DIFFERENCE AND CONNECTION BETWEEN KNOWLEDGE, UNDERSTANDING AND WISDOM

You are learning a great deal from this book, which aims to help you leverage the power of the seasons of your life. As we conclude this chapter, I would like to explore the concepts of knowledge, understanding, and wisdom: their differences and connections.

Firstly, what is the meaning of knowledge, understanding, and wisdom?

Knowledge refers to the information and facts that a person has acquired through learning, experience, or education. It involves knowing about a particular subject, topic, or area of interest. Knowledge can be factual and is often based on data, evidence, or information that can be taught or learned. It represents what we know.

While a significant portion of knowledge comes from learning or experience, a percentage comes through instinct or spiritual means. As Pierre Teilhard de Chardin, the French philosopher, wisely stated, *'We are not human beings having a spiritual experience. We are spiritual beings having a human experience.'* We possess an ability that transcends the physical realm, allowing us to know things without necessarily studying them. Hence, knowledge is considered one of the gifts of the spirit by Paul. This, however, does not negate the importance of studying and learning; instead, it emphasises the significance of harnessing both.

Take, for example, the story of Pharaoh in ancient Egypt. He gained knowledge of future events through a dream and not by reading about it. This highlights one way to acquire knowledge. Similarly, Daniel and his friends, despite their talent for interpreting dreams, had to undergo a three-year education at the University of Babylon. Their knowledge did not come without studying. This underscores the importance of reading and studying, as these provide the foundation for understanding and the wisdom necessary for achieving success, as we will soon see.

Now, what is understanding?

Understanding goes beyond mere knowledge. It involves comprehending, interpreting, and grasping the meaning or significance of information or knowledge. It's about making connections, seeing relationships, and being able to explain or apply what one knows. Understanding reflects how we process and make sense of knowledge.

For instance, consider Pharaoh's dream about the fat and thin cows. Pharaoh recounted the dream to his magicians while Joseph was in prison. Pharaoh had knowledge of the dream but did not understand it. Similarly, when he related it to them, his magicians acquired the knowledge of the dream, but they could not discern its meaning. This illustrates the distinction between knowledge and understanding.

When Joseph was summoned, the dream was narrated to him as well, but he possessed a gift that surpassed that of the magicians. He didn't just gain the knowledge of the dream; he understood it. Joseph could interpret the dream and extract its meaning, demonstrating what is referred to as understanding.

Have you ever read a book or passage without knowing its meaning or significance? We need to understand a subject to take advantage of it fully. Knowledge lacks utility without understanding. The story of the biblical eunuch further illustrates this point, as he read the book of Isaiah but failed to understand it. When Philip asked if he comprehended what he read, the eunuch replied, **'How can I unless someone guides me?'**(24)

Now, Joseph could have simply interpreted the dreams and left. What do you think would have happened to the people without anyone providing the proper insight to prepare for the upcoming famine if he had done that? This is where wisdom comes into play. Now, what is wisdom?

Wisdom is the capacity to make sound judgments, apply knowledge and understanding to real-life situations, and navigate complex challenges. Wisdom involves discernment, practical insight, and the ability to make informed and impactful decisions.

Joseph provided a solution to the foreseen challenge. He advised the creation of a reserve from the seven years of plenty, which would help them weather the storm of the impending famine. Joseph stressed that Pharaoh should appoint an administrator to oversee the food reserves during the years of abundance. Joseph's wisdom didn't stop at interpretation; it extended to practical action and leadership in implementing a plan that saved Egypt from disaster. **Wisdom provides solutions, and often, you are not compensated for your knowledge but for the solutions you offer.** Wisdom is the ultimate goal you should aspire to. Imagine if Joseph had been clueless about the solution to the dream. Take a moment to imagine this. The purpose of knowledge and understanding is to provide a foundation for wisdom and, consequently, solutions and success.

He proposed a twenty per cent reserve, unlike the traditional tithe (ten per cent) he was accustomed to. **Wisdom does not always follow the path of common knowledge and tradition.** I recently met a senior colleague who intrigued me with his understanding. He asked, **"How curious are you about life?"** He emphasised the importance of curiosity in achieving success. "You should be willing to question tradition and ask why things were done the way they were done. By seeking to understand why, you may discover insights others have overlooked." he continued.

He shared an anecdote from his childhood when he unscrewed a lightbulb at less than ten years old and ventured into a well out of sheer curiosity. He acknowledged that pursuing curiosity might lead to taking a risky path, which could even be life-threatening. However, he stressed that it's essential not to remain ignorant.

In conclusion, wisdom transcends mere knowledge or understanding; it represents the practical application of knowledge and understanding to achieve positive and far-reaching outcomes. Always consider what solutions you can proffer from what you know and understand. Remember that one can be a professor in a subject yet remain impoverished if they do not apply their knowledge.

It has been an incredible journey thus far as we conclude the second season, the spring of opportunity. It's time to transition into the third season, the Summer of Growth and Progress. I welcome you to the next chapter of this book. It's important to note that these seasons do not necessarily occur in a fixed sequence. Winter doesn't have to precede spring or any other season, and experiencing a season in the past doesn't mean it won't reappear in your life. Some people associate these seasons with age, but that's not the primary focus of this book. I commend you for reading this far. Send me feedback here [mailto:pnuxelconsulting@gmail.com] or recommend this book to another person. Feel free to go ahead with any that resonates with you. It is time to move on to the next chapter.

Chapter Six

PROTECTING THE SUMMER OF GROWTH AND PROGRESS

"The best way to predict your future is to create it." -
Abraham Lincoln

Welcome, dear readers, to the next chapter of our journey through the seasons of life. We've come a long way, having traversed the harsh terrains of winter's challenges and basked in the budding opportunities of spring. Now, as we turn the page to the next chapter, we enter the splendid season of summer – a season of growth and progress.

But before diving into the sunny summer world, let's take a moment to appreciate how far we've come. Think back to the icy winter chill when we discussed facing life's hardships head-on, finding resilience, and preparing for the brighter days ahead. Then, we ventured into spring, learning to recognise and seize the opportunities surrounding us.

Now, summer is upon us. It's a season of warmth when the days stretch longer. It's known for growth and progress following the seedtime. Your seeds are now sprouting, and it's time to nurture and safeguard your plants. In this chapter, we'll delve into how you can play the roles of both a gardener and a guardian, tending and protecting your growth, progress, and hard-earned successes. It's a time to take on the nurturing care of a mother and the protective role of a father, metaphorically speaking.

BE A GARDENER AND GUARDIAN

I trust that you are actively seizing the spring of opportunities by maintaining a positive mindset and working to achieve the success you deserve. As you sow your seeds, it's crucial to understand that planting alone doesn't guarantee a bountiful harvest. You might wonder why – and the reason is quite simple. Just as your seeds sprout and grow, pests and insects are attracted to your garden, seeking to feed on and destroy your growing crops.

So, as you transition into the summer of growth and progress, you must not only put on the hat of a gardener but also that of a guardian. You cannot be solely a gardener; you have the added responsibility of safeguarding your growth and progress. Neglecting to protect your advancement can lead to losing the success you rightfully deserve.

Consider the story of the diligent farmer who, after sowing his seeds with optimism, tended his crops, watered and weeded, and noticed destructive pests threatening to devour his crops. The farmer had worked tirelessly and invested in his crops, but now he needs to act to stop these invaders from ruining his labour.

In his commitment to gardening and guarding, he sought advice and learned various methods to protect his crops. With persistence and creativity, he developed deterrents that kept the pests at bay. The diligent farmer's garden thrived, yielding a bountiful harvest that rewarded his hard work and careful protection.

Like this farmer, you, too, must nurture your endeavours while guarding them against potential threats. Being a gardener and guardian means proactively safeguarding your progress from the pests that might attempt to diminish the harvest of your hard work. This diligence will ensure that you not only sow the seeds of success but also reap the full benefits of your efforts.

As Winston Churchill said, *"Success is not final, failure is not fatal: It is the courage to continue that counts."* Your courage to act as a gardener and a guardian ensures your success isn't temporary or easily lost. The following season may bring new challenges, but your readiness to nurture and protect your progress guarantees you're well-prepared to embrace the harvest that lies ahead.

NURTURE AS A MOTHER AND PROTECT AS A FATHER

During the summer, you'll find your plans and aspirations blossoming. Like in a thriving garden, you've carefully sown the seeds of your dreams and ambitions, nurtured them, and watched them grow. But as your efforts flourish, so do the challenges and threats, like pests drawn to a garden in full bloom.

This season's lesson teaches us to approach our growing success with the dual roles of nurturing as a mother and protecting as a father. Picture a thriving family where the mother provides love, care, and sustenance while the father stands to guard, safeguarding against potential dangers. These two roles are essential to the prosperity of any household, and they apply to our journey in life, too.

A mother's role extends beyond caring for her children; it also includes protection. Take, for instance, my neighbour's dog, which recently gave birth. Despite her generally friendly nature, she became remarkably protective of her puppies in the first few days after giving birth. She saw everyone as a potential intruder, and her commitment wasn't just to provide care but also to fiercely protect her offspring. Have you ever witnessed a mother's fierce determination to shield her young from harm?

Likewise, a father is capable of assuming the role of a nurturer. The point I'm emphasising here is that, as you nurture your seeds of greatness, it's equally essential to shield them from potential threats, be it external factors or destructive habits that can undermine your journey to success. Don't allow these pests to take root; instead, nip them in the bud. You should not be ignorant of the pests, just as the bible story illustrates that while the gardener slept, the enemy came and sowed weeds among the crops.

When you're diligently planting and nurturing your dreams during the initial stages, you may attract little attention. You blend in with the crowd virtually unnoticed. However, as your success blossoms, you become noticeable, and adversaries will inevitably emerge, seeking to exploit your achievements. You must stand your ground against any enemy that threatens your harvest and the great success you're cultivating. Remember, as the protective mother dog illustrated above, guarding your progress is as important as nurturing it.

PROTECT YOURSELF FROM YOURSELF.

As we delve deeper into the summer of growth and progress, we encounter a unique challenge – the need to protect our advancements. While it's natural to assume that we're primarily responsible for safeguarding our growth and success from external threats and intruders, the first enemy we must shield our progress from is ourselves. Indeed, the importance of conquering ourselves is eloquently conveyed by Plato, who stated, ***"The first and greatest victory is to conquer yourself; to be conquered by yourself is of all things most shameful and vile."*** At times, you can become your own worst adversaries. Often, not external factors hinder your progress but your thoughts, behaviours, and, most importantly, your habits.

We've witnessed individuals dismantle their empires of success through their own hands by their unchecked habits and appetites. These tendencies may go unnoticed when they're not in the spotlight or have no achievements to boast about. However, as soon as they rise above the crowd and become a figure of note, those seemingly insignificant habits can prove vital to determine the sustenance of their growth, success, and progress. It's wise to protect yourself from your actions by nipping undesirable habits in the bud; as an African adage suggests, ***"The branches of an Iroko tree are pruned when it's still a seedling; otherwise, it will grow wild and require a sacrifice."*** In other words, it's better to address an issue while still manageable.

Just as self-discipline is vital for planting your seeds, it's equally essential for nurturing and protecting your crops. Don't permit yourself to live without boundaries. Establish a value system that will serve as a protective shield for your hard-earned success and efforts.

Consider, for a moment, that you are working on a garden. You've put in the hard work, meticulously planting your seeds and nurturing your crops. The soil is rich, the sun is warm, and everything is thriving. However, out of the blue, you begin plucking the very seedlings you've cultivated, or worse, pouring crude oil into the soil under the mistaken belief that it will help. This vividly illustrates what a lack of self-boundaries and self-discipline looks like.

Joseph's story offers a valuable lesson in this regard. As he ascended the ladder of success, he resisted the temptation posed by his master's wife. His restraint came at the cost of his comfort but was essential to protect his growth and progress.

Take an inventory of your habits and make adjustments as necessary so that you can protect yourself from yourself in the summer of growth and progress.

PROTECT YOURSELF FROM EXTERNAL INTRUDERS.

As we have seen before, the summer of growth and progress is a time when your hard work, efforts, and determination start to bear fruit. Your garden is lush, and your crops are flourishing. But, as any seasoned gardener knows, a thriving garden is an attractive haven for all sorts of external intruders. In our context, these intruders can be distractions, negative influences, or external challenges that threaten to impede your growth and progress.

One significant external intruder is distraction. Think of your focus and attention as precious resources. Just as you wouldn't want pests to devour your thriving crops, you don't want distractions to consume your valuable time and energy. These distractions can come in many forms, from the constant ping of your phone to the lure of time-wasting activities. They divert your attention from your goals and hinder your continuous progress.

Distractions may not always stem from the above sources; they can also manifest in the form of people seeking your attention because you're standing out. While they may express the desire to associate with you, they may be time-wasters who can negatively influence you. You must remain vigilant and protect your progress from such individuals. Strive to surround yourself with individuals with a positive mindset, and extend your assistance to those you can genuinely support. **Understanding this fundamental truth about life is crucial – you cannot assist everyone.**

You must establish boundaries against these distractions to protect your summer of growth. Consider allocating specific times for focused work and ensuring those around you understand your commitment to your goals. You can safeguard your garden of progress by recognising these distractions and actively working to minimise them.

As I wrap up the discussion on distractions, I want to emphasise the power of saying "no." I must admit that I struggled with this concept initially. It felt uncomfortable to turn down tasks or requests, especially when I was capable of handling them. However, I soon realised that I get choked with saying "yes" to everything, and also, when I say "no" to one thing, I'm essentially saying "yes" to something else. This insight has been invaluable, and we'll delve deeper into this idea in the upcoming section of this chapter.

Negative influences are another type of external intruder. Just as a gardener must protect his plants from harmful pests, you must guard your aspirations from influences that can hinder your growth. Negative influences can include people who are pessimistic, unsupportive, or critics of your dreams. Their words and attitudes can cast a shadow on your sunny season of growth.

Author and motivational speaker Jim Rohn aptly noted, ***"You are the average of the five people you spend the most time with."*** This statement underscores the profound influence that those around us can have on our lives. To protect your growth garden, be mindful of the company you keep. Surround yourself with individuals who uplift, inspire, and support your aspirations. In this way, you create a positive and nurturing environment for your progress.

As your summer season unfolds, you might encounter external circumstances beyond your control. Like sudden storms, they can threaten your progress. Just as a gardener protects their garden from harsh weather, you must take measures to weather such external circumstances. As the saying goes, *"Hope for the best and be prepared for the worst"*. Instead of viewing them as insurmountable roadblocks, consider them opportunities to develop resilience and adaptability.

Just as a gardener uses various methods to protect their garden from intruders, you can employ strategies to shield your progress from external distractions, negative influences, and circumstances beyond your control. By cultivating this protective mindset, you ensure that your summer season remains a time of flourishing growth and unwavering progress.

LEARN TO SAY "NO."

One significant aspect of safeguarding our progress is our ability to set boundaries, which involves learning to say "no" strategically.

Imagine your summer season as your flourishing garden, teeming with beautiful and valuable plants. However, weeds may seek to infiltrate your garden. If left unchecked, these weeds can choke your plants, hindering their growth and stealing vital nutrients. Similarly, numerous requests and tasks may come your way in the summer of growth. Some are like the precious crops you've nurtured, aligned with your goals and values. Others, however, resemble weeds, sapping your time, energy, and focus, leaving you exhausted and hindering your progress.

Just as a diligent gardener distinguishes between the crops and weeds, you must discern between requests that align with your purpose and those that divert you from your path. Learning to say "no" is not a hostile act;

it's a strategic choice to guard and guide your progress. As Warren Buffett wisely stated, *"The difference between successful people and very successful people is that very successful people say 'no' to almost everything."*

It's essential to understand that saying "no" is not an act of selfishness but a commitment to your journey's purpose and direction. Every "yes" to a request or task is, in essence, a "no" to something else, including time dedicated to your essential goals. Like in the garden, your resources, such as time and energy, are finite. You must allocate them thoughtfully to ensure that your most valuable crops continue to thrive.

Consider the story of the ten virgins from the Bible who were waiting for the bridegroom's arrival. Five were wise and brought extra oil for their lamps, while the others were foolish and unprepared. When the bridegroom's arrival was delayed, the lamps of the foolish virgins began to run out of oil, and they turned to the wise virgins for help. The wise virgins, though compassionate, recognised the importance of saying "no" in this situation. They refused to share their oil, knowing that if they did, they would find themselves in a similar crisis and fail with the others. Do you get that? It is wise to turn down what will clog your wheel of progress or what will take your focus away from your success.

In the same way, you must discern between what will propel your journey forward and what might extinguish your success. Learning to say "no" to tasks and requests that divert you from your goals ensures that you remain adequately prepared for your growth and success. By setting boundaries and prioritising what truly matters, you protect your progress and guard against becoming overwhelmed.

Remember that the more you learn to say "no" when necessary, the more you can say "yes" to your dreams and aspirations. It's not about rejecting opportunities but about embracing them in the real sense. This way, you guide your summer of growth towards the fruitful harvest you've been nurturing rather than allowing it to be overrun by the weeds of distraction and overcommitment.

PROTECT YOUR VALUES

What do you think of this book as we continue our journey through the summer of growth and progress? Your feedback is invaluable, so feel free to share your thoughts with me at [pnuxelconsulting@gmail.com]. Your input will help me refine this work and make it even more beneficial.

Now, let's delve into another crucial aspect of sustaining your growth and progress: protecting your values. Your values serve as the bedrock of your character, and safeguarding them is vital for lasting success. As John Wooden rightly said, ***"Ability may get you to the top, but it takes character to keep you there."*** As you progress and ascend in your endeavours, your character becomes increasingly evident, unlike in the past when it goes unnoticed.

Therefore, building strong character and protecting it is imperative, especially during your summer of growth and progress. Of course, you embrace great values even before you get to the summer of your life.

In this season of growth, your character will face various tests, and one area where this may be evident is your financial integrity. You might have had little financial responsibility in the past, but as you grow and transition into the summer of your success, you may find yourself managing substantial financial resources. Now, your financial integrity is under scrutiny. It's up to you to protect this value, ensuring that honesty and integrity remain central to your dealings with money.

You might get away with financial misappropriation in the short term, but who knows when hidden actions will come to the limelight. The cost of such revelations can be far more significant than the mishandled money. Therefore, safeguarding your financial integrity is essential for sustaining your success.

Upholding your financial integrity, especially when the stakes are high, serves as a testament to your character and reflects your unwavering commitment to your values.

Protecting your values is not limited to financial integrity alone; it extends to all the values that you hold dear, such as family values and sexual integrity, among others. Drawing wisdom from the Apostle Peter, we learned the importance of diligently adding virtues like faith, knowledge, self-control, perseverance, godliness, brotherly kindness, and love to our lives, among other values. If you nurture these values and let them flourish, you'll find yourself neither barren nor unfruitful.

Protecting your values isn't just a passive exercise; it's an active commitment to upholding your principles and virtues in all circumstances. In the summer of growth and progress, your values are the compass guiding your actions. Remember that your character is your legacy, and it's in this season that your true character will shine brightly. Embrace your values, protect them fiercely, and let them lead you towards lasting success and fulfilment.

SAFEGUARDING YOUR MOST PRECIOUS RESOURCE: YOUR TIME

In your journey through life, you might have noticed that, initially, when you were planting seeds and nurturing your growth, there were very few eyes on you. You were like a small plant sprouting in a vast field. Your actions, your choices, and your efforts all went relatively unnoticed. But as you transition into your summer of growth and progress, things are changing. Your hard work and dedication have brought forth fruits. Your small plant has grown into a substantial tree with fruits. And suddenly, you find yourself in the spotlight. People are drawn to you, curious about your success, and eager to be part of your journey.

However, with this newfound attention comes a challenge, a battle you must win – the fight to protect your most precious resource: your time. This resource is finite. Once time is gone, it cannot be replaced or reclaimed. As William Penn wisely stated, *"Time is what we want most, but what we use worst."* Your success story has made you a magnet for various requests, distractions, and individuals who want your time for meaningful and meaningless purposes.

The stakes are high as you bask in the summer of your growth and progress. You'll face more and more demands on your time and attention. You must learn to filter through these requests and protect your time, ensuring that it is invested wisely in the activities that continue to nurture your success. If you allow time to slip through your fingers, you risk opening the door to intruders who may steal and squander your time on unimportant and unimpactful things. It's no longer about merely managing your time; it's about protecting it.

One of the quotes that exemplifies the importance of guarding your time is from Jim Rohn: *"Time is more valuable than money. You can get more money, but you cannot get more time."* Your time is the currency of life, and how you spend it determines the value of your existence. When you were planting your seeds and nurturing your growth, you likely had more control over your time, but as you progress, this control becomes more challenging.

Here are some tips to guard your time:

1. **Prioritise and Say No:** To guard your time effectively, you must master the art of prioritisation. Recognise the tasks, people, and activities that align with your goals and are crucial to your growth. Filter out those that aren't. It's essential to realise that saying "no" to certain requests or distractions is not a rejection; it's a strategic choice to safeguard your time and keep the focus on what truly matters. Just as Warren Buffet wisely stated, *"The difference between successful people and really successful*

people is that really successful people say no to almost everything."

2. **Set Boundaries:** Creating boundaries is another vital strategy. These boundaries define when, how, and with whom you're willing to share your time. They can shield you from the onslaught of unnecessary interruptions and help maintain your focus. The ability to say, "I'm available during these hours" or "I prioritise my mornings for focused work" helps set expectations and protects your valuable time. The Pomodoro Technique comes in handy here too.

3. **Leverage Time Management Tools:** Time management tools, such as calendars and task lists, can be beneficial. They assist in structuring your day, prioritising tasks, and minimising time wastage. As Peter Drucker aptly said, *"Until we can manage time, we can manage nothing else."* These tools help you allocate

your time efficiently so you remain in control even as the demands on your time increase.

4. **Learn to Delegate:** Delegation is a skill that successful individuals often master. It means entrusting certain tasks to others, freeing you to focus on high-impact activities. As a leader in your journey, this skill will be valuable in ensuring you protect your time for the most significant contributions only you can make.

5. **Discover More in My Book:** In my book, '**From Overwhelmed to Organized: A Time Management Blueprint for Busy Professionals**,' I delve even deeper into time management. You can find it at [https://www.amazon.co.uk/dp/B0BSTYWVHZ], your favourite retailer, or contact me at [pnuxelconsulting@gmail.com].

Your summer of growth and progress brings both the rewards of your hard work and the challenge of protecting your most precious resource – your time. As you continue to flourish, remember the wisdom of Ralph Waldo Emerson: ***"This time, like all times, is a very good one if we but know what to do with it."*** Knowing what to do with your time is the key to nurturing and preserving your success.

It is time to move to the next season, and we will do justice to that in the next chapter. Let's get going.

Chapter Seven

EMBRACING THE AUTUMN OF HARVEST

He who continually goes forth weeping, bearing seed for sowing, shall doubtless come again with rejoicing, bringing his sheaves with him. Psalm 126:6

Before we delve into the pages of "Embracing the Autumn of Harvest," I want to take a moment to commend you for embarking on this enlightening journey through the pages of this book. We've navigated the winter of challenges, seizing the spring of opportunities and protecting the summer of growth and progress. The fact that you're here, having navigated these seasons alongside, is a testament to your commitment to personal development.

As we step into this chapter, "Embracing the Autumn of Harvest," we've reached a season where your seeds are yielding fruits. Autumn, both in nature and in life, is a time of reward and harvest. It is a time to celebrate and enjoy the returns of your dedication, resilience and hard work.

In this chapter, we'll explore how to embrace this season of your life fully. As we do so, remember that each chapter of this book is designed to help you leverage the unique power of each season in your life.

REAPING WHAT YOU'VE SOWN: THE LAW OF THE HARVEST

As we enter autumn, we are greeted with the universal truth that *"you cannot reap what you have not sown."* This ancient wisdom transcends time, cultures, and generations, echoing the fundamental law of the harvest. It speaks to the essence of effort, patience, and the direct relationship between the seeds you plant and the fruits you ultimately enjoy.

Autumn is when we witness the tangible outcomes of our actions, intentions, and decisions from the preceding seasons. Just as a farmer carefully selects and sows the right seeds, you, too, are the cultivator of your life's garden. Your choices, actions, and investments serve as the seeds that determine your future harvest. If you desire a fruitful autumn, it's essential to reflect on the quality of the seeds you've sown during the preceding seasons.

Imagine an apple orchard where a diligent farmer meticulously nurtures each tree. He tends to their needs, ensuring they receive adequate sunlight, water, and care. He diligently plants the seeds in the spring and watches as they grow. Throughout the summer, he protects the trees and provides the necessary care. As autumn arrives, he is rewarded with a bountiful harvest of crisp, juicy apples. The farmer understands that without his dedicated efforts in the preceding seasons, the apples he enjoys in autumn would never have come to fruition.

In life, your actions mirror the diligent farmer. The career choices you make, the relationships you nurture, the knowledge you acquire, and the values you uphold are all the seeds you sow. As you embrace the autumn of your life, the fruits you reap directly reflect your earlier efforts. Just as a well-cultivated apple tree yields sweet fruit, a carefully tended to and thoughtfully nurtured life offers the richness of a bountiful harvest.

This principle emphasises that the results of your experience are the consequences of your actions. It's a reminder that life operates on the principle of cause and effect. The effort you invest in your goals, the care you extend to your relationships, and the commitment to your values ultimately determine the quality of your harvest. As you navigate this chapter, consider the seeds you've sown and the bountiful harvest you hope to gather. In life, autumn is your opportunity to savour the fruits of your labour, recognising that you cannot reap what you have not sown.

You cannot sow an apple seed and hope to harvest a pineapple; this goes against the law of harvest.

TAKE RESPONSIBILITY FOR YOUR HARVEST

As we have seen, autumn represents the culmination of your efforts when you stand before the harvest of your choices, actions, and decisions. It's a time to take responsibility for your harvest and a moment for self-reflection, a chance to acknowledge your role in shaping your destiny. This section titled "Take Responsibility for Your Harvest" underscores a profound truth – your life is a garden you've tended, and the quality of your harvest is intrinsically linked to your choices.

As Abraham Lincoln wisely said, *"You cannot escape the responsibility of tomorrow by evading it today."* Many people find it easy to place blame on external factors for their life's outcomes. They point fingers at their parents, the economy, the government, or even cosmic forces beyond their control. They blame every other thing except themselves. The list of scapegoats is endless, and it's convenient to shift the responsibility for their circumstances elsewhere. However, **true growth and maturity begin when you are ready to take responsibility for your life.** Taking ownership of your harvest is very important. Whether you achieve a bountiful harvest or otherwise, you should have the courage to take responsibility for the outcome. Doing so enables you to make the necessary adjustments for your desired change and success. Don't be too timid to take ownership of your mistakes, strengths, and achievements.

Brian Tracy's personal narrative offers a compelling example of the transformative power of taking responsibility for your harvest. He once found himself trapped in a cycle of long working hours and meagre income, struggling to meet his financial obligations. It was a turning point for him when he recognised that he was responsible for his finances. By embracing the responsibility for his harvest, he transformed his life from financial hardship to remarkable success.

You may not have control over every external circumstance in your life, but you do have dominion over your choices, mindset, and actions. Instead of attempting to change the people and conditions around you, the focus should shift to changing yourself. Your life's harvest directly reflects the seeds you've sown. **If you aspire to change your life, begin by changing your mindset.**

The power of responsibility is not limited to your past actions and decisions; it also extends to your future. It is the key that opens the door to self-improvement, growth, and transformation. Taking responsibility for your harvest is not an act of self-blame but an act of self-empowerment. It means recognising that while you may not control every circumstance, you have the power to influence the outcome by taking ownership of your choices.

As you continue to navigate the autumn of your life, remember that each day offers the opportunity to accept responsibility for your harvest. Your decisions, actions, and mindset shape your life's garden. Embrace this responsibility as a catalyst for personal growth, success, and fulfilling your aspirations.

NAVIGATING THE SHADOWS OF IMPOSTER SYNDROME

As you stand amidst the abundant harvest of your life's work, it's essential to acknowledge that the journey through the autumn of harvest can be peppered with the shadows of self-doubt and insecurity. Imposter Syndrome, aptly named, is a phenomenon that often accompanies significant success. It's the persistent feeling that you don't deserve the accomplishments, recognition, or accolades you've earned and that you'll be exposed as a fraud one day.

Maya Angelou once stated, *"I have written eleven books, but each time I think, 'uh oh, they're going to find out now. I've run a game on everybody, and they're going to find me out.'"* This sentiment is echoed by accomplished individuals who, despite their numerous achievements, grapple with feelings of inadequacy and the fear of being unmasked as impostors.

Imposter Syndrome thrives in the hearts of those who have scaled great heights. It's not exclusive to novices, nor does it discriminate based on experience. It's an equal opportunity intruder that can creep into the minds of seasoned professionals, entrepreneurs, artists, and leaders.

The paradox of Imposter Syndrome is that it often affects those who are the most competent. High-achieving individuals often hold themselves to high standards, a driving force behind their success. Yet, this attribute can make them feel like they are falling short despite impressive accomplishments.

A quote by Albert Einstein provides an insightful perspective on this internal struggle: *"The exaggerated esteem in which my lifework is held makes me very ill at ease. I feel compelled to think of myself as an involuntary swindler."* This illustrates how success can magnify the fear of being exposed as an impostor, creating an internal conflict between one's true abilities and the perception of others.

The key to conquering Imposter Syndrome in the autumn of your life is self-awareness and self-compassion. First, recognise that these feelings are common among high-achievers. You are not alone in your battle against this internal shadow. Second, be compassionate to yourself, acknowledging that you've earned your place among your peers.

Remember that your road to success was lined with challenges, self-doubt, fear, courage, patience and persistence. You have sown the seeds of your endeavours during the spring and diligently tended to them during the summer. Your harvest results from your diligence and dedication and, of course, God smiling on your input.

Imposter Syndrome may cast shadows in the autumn of your harvest, but these shadows cannot diminish your achievements. As you navigate this season, bask in the warmth of self-recognition and the fruits of your labour. Embrace that you are not an impostor but a skilled gardener of your success story. Every season, including autumn, has unique challenges and triumphs. The key is to recognise that the imposter syndrome is merely a passing cloud, while your accomplishments are the enduring fruits of your labour.

LEARN TO ENJOY THE FRUITS OF YOUR LABOR

As you stand amidst the field of your autumn harvest, the sense of accomplishment and fulfilment should be not just acknowledged but celebrated. Yet, there's a common tendency, especially among the relentless achievers, to keep pushing forward without pausing to relish the fruits of their labour.

Your journey through life's seasons has brought you to the point where you can finally enjoy the rewards of your hard work and diligence. However, this transition is often met with challenges for many. Some struggle with the guilt of taking time off or a relentless drive to keep achieving, while others may feel they have not yet accomplished enough.

"No one on his deathbed ever said, 'I wish I had spent more time at the office.'" believed to be said by Paul Tsongas, a former United States Senator. This notion underscores the importance of balancing your professional and personal life, and your work life and harvest. All the success you've achieved, the hurdles you've overcome, and the seeds you've sown in the spring and tended to during the summer have led to this moment – the opportunity to savour the sweetness of your autumn harvest.

Consider your accomplishments as the ripe, delicious fruits of your labour. Take time to relish your achievements and appreciate the journey that has brought you here. This moment is not just about tangible success but also about the experiences, the lessons learned, and the growth that has unfolded during your pursuit.

Enjoying your harvest is not a call to complacency but a reminder that finding balance in your life is crucial. It's about recognising that all work and no play not only make Jack a dull boy but can also make him an exhausted, stressed, and unfulfilled individual. **Pursuing excellence is commendable, but not at the expense of your well-being, self-satisfaction and fulfilment.**

In the words of John Lubbock, *"Rest is not idleness, and to lie sometimes on the grass under trees on a summer's day, listening to the murmur of the water, or watching the clouds float across the sky, is by no means a waste of time."* This echoes the sentiment that rest and enjoyment are integral to a fulfilling life.

The autumn season offers you a unique opportunity to enjoy your achievements, spend quality time with your loved ones, and pursue the activities that bring you joy. It's about creating a life where the fruits of your labour are not just on your plate but enjoyed and experienced in the richness of your relationships, the joy of your hobbies, and the tranquillity of moments well spent.

The autumn of your life's harvest should be embraced with open arms and a contented heart. Savour the fruits of your labour, for they are the essence of your life's work and why you've journeyed through the seasons. It's not merely a time to rest; it's a time to live and appreciate the beauty of the life you've cultivated.

EMBRACE THE SEASONS, HARVEST YOUR SUCCESS

As we conclude this enlightening journey through the chapters of "**Leveraging the Power of Seasons: Understanding and Taking Advantage of the Four Seasons of Life,**" it's crucial to understand that life's journey is a beautiful blend of seasons. Just as nature gracefully shifts from the harsh grasp of winter to the rejuvenation of spring, followed by the flourishing growth of summer, and ultimately to the bountiful harvest of autumn, our lives, too, follow this beautiful and evolving rhythm.

Life is not a monotonous, never-ending summer or an eternal winter of challenges. It's a dynamic and ever-changing cycle. As you've walked through these pages, you've gleaned the wisdom of embracing change and personal growth. You've discovered that even in the darkest winter, there's hope and a path to seizing the spring of opportunities.

In navigating life's winter, you've found strength in adversity, learning that character and faith are forged in the fires of hardship. Seizing the spring has become an art as you've cultivated a positive mindset and, more importantly, learned the keys to recognising and taking advantage of opportunities.

The concept of "seed time" has become ingrained in your understanding. Like a well-tended garden, you've realised that life requires nurturing and protection. You've learned to say "no" when necessary and safeguard your values and precious time.

Now, as you step into the autumn of your journey, remember the Law of the Harvest: "You cannot reap what you have not sown." Take full responsibility for your harvest and navigate the shadows of imposter syndrome. The fruits of your labour are here, and it's time to savour them.

So, embrace the seasons of life, harvest your success, and know that this is just the beginning. The lessons you've gained from each season will continue to guide you through life's ever-turning wheel.

As we come to the end of this book, I would love to hear your thoughts and experiences with the book. Please leave a review on your favourite book retailer platform or send your feedback via email to [pnuxelconsulting@gmail.com]. I will greatly value your input and look forward to hearing from you.

And if you're eager to explore more insights, consider delving into my Amazon bestseller, **"From Overwhelmed to Organized: A Time Management Blueprint for Busy Professionals."** You can find it here: [https://www.amazon.co.uk/dp/B0BSVHBLFV].

Plus, I have a library of other enlightening books waiting for you. Discover more at [https://amazon.co.uk/Toyin-Obafemi/e/B081TLJKH7].

Congratulations and cheers to a successful and incredible journey!

.

Unlock Your Potential: Discover the Transformative Power of My Other Books

Are you ready to take control of your life and achieve your dreams? Look no further. In addition to "From Overwhelmed to Organised: A Time Management Blueprint for Busy Professionals," I have also written other books to help guide you on your journey to success.

In **"49 Words on Marble,"** I share wisdom and inspiration through powerful affirmations and motivational quotes for men and women, young and old. Positive mindset quotes to start your day and improve your life.

"How to Live Above Circumstances" teaches you how to be in control of your life and overcome any obstacle that may come your way. **"The Beatitudes"** explores the concept of living a life of happiness, prosperity, liberty, and blessedness.

In **"Write a Book Without Breaking a Sweat,"** I share the secrets to writing a book easily, making the process less daunting and more enjoyable. **"The Role of Graphic Design and Technology in Writing"** delves into the blogging world and how to develop a successful blog harnessing technology.

Take advantage of these transformative books. Check them out today by visiting my website [https://toyinobafemi.com.ng], Amazon kindle store [https://www.amazon.com/Toyin-H.-Obafemi/e/B081TLJKH7], or searching for them in your favourite bookstores. And remember, apart from the ones mentioned here, you can get all my other books to help you achieve your goals and live the life you deserve.

THE AUTHOR

Dr. Toyin Obafemi is an author, coach, and medical doctor, currently serving as a Senior Registrar in Internal Medicine with an interest in Dermatology.

With a commitment to helping people live a better life, Dr. Obafemi has authored more than ten impactful books published and distributed globally. His latest book, **"From Overwhelmed to Organized: A Time Management Blueprint for Busy Professionals,"** reflects an insightful understanding of the challenges those leading demanding professional lives face. Drawing from personal experiences as a busy physician, author, coach, and digital solutions consultant, this book has earned recognition as an Amazon best-seller.

Having experienced the ups and downs of life, Dr. Obafemi understands the common challenges we face in navigating life's complexities. That's why he has written another book, **"Leveraging the Power of**

Seasons: Understanding and Taking Advantage of the Four Seasons of Life," to help readers make the most of the twists and turns of life.

Beyond his professional pursuits, Dr Obafemi finds fulfilment in his role as a dedicated spouse to Temitope and a loving father to two children, Oreofe and Inioluwa. This holistic approach to life underscores his value on personal relationships and balance amidst his numerous commitments.

REFERENCES

1. Genesis 8:22 "While the earth remains, Seedtime and harvest, Cold and heat, Winter and summer, And day and night Shall not cease." | New King James Version (NKJV) | Download The Bible App Now [Internet]. [cited 2023 Nov 11]. Available from: https://www.bible.com/bible/114/GEN.8.22.NKJV

2. Psalms 30:5 For His anger is but for a moment, His favor is for life; Weeping may endure for a night, But joy comes in the morning. | New King James Version (NKJV) | Download The Bible App Now [Internet]. [cited 2023 Nov 11]. Available from: https://www.bible.com/bible/114/PSA.30.5.NKJV

3. 1 Corinthians 10:13 The temptations in your life are no different from what others experience. And God is faithful. He will not allow the temptation to be more than you can stand. When you are tempted, he will show you a | New Living Translation (NLT) | Download The Bible App Now [Internet]. [cited 2023 Nov 11]. Available from: https://www.bible.com/bible/116/1CO.10.13.NLT

4. Luke 22:31-32 "Simon, stay on your toes. Satan has tried his best to separate all of you from me, like chaff from wheat. Simon, I've prayed for you in particular that you not give in or give out. When you have come | The Message (MSG) | Download The

Bible App Now [Internet]. [cited 2023 Nov 11]. Available from: https://www.bible.com/bible/97/LUK.22.31.MSG

5. Matthew 7:7 "Ask, and it will be given to you; seek, and you will find; knock, and it will be opened to you. I New King James Version (NKJV) I Download The Bible App Now [Internet]. [cited 2023 Nov 11]. Available from: https://www.bible.com/bible/114/MAT.7.7.NKJV

6. Isaiah 43:2 When you pass through the waters, I will be with you; And through the rivers, they shall not overflow you. When you walk through the fire, you shall not be burned, Nor shall the flame scorch you. I New King James Version (NKJV) I Download The Bible App Now [Internet]. [cited 2023 Nov 11]. Available from: https://www.bible.com/bible/114/ISA.43.2.NKJV

7. Proverbs 24:10 If you faint in the day of adversity, Your strength is small. I New King James Version (NKJV) I Download The Bible App Now [Internet]. [cited 2023 Nov 11]. Available from: https://www.bible.com/bible/114/PRO.24.10.NKJV

8. Job 13:15 Though He slay me, yet will I trust Him. Even so, I will defend my own ways before Him. I New King James Version (NKJV) I Download The Bible App Now [Internet]. [cited 2023 Nov 11]. Available from: https://www.bible.com/bible/114/JOB.13.15.NKJV

9. 1 Peter 4:12-13 Friends, when life gets really difficult, don't jump to the conclusion that God isn't on the job. Instead, be glad that you are in the very thick of what Christ experienced. This is a spiritual refini | The Message (MSG) | Download The Bible App Now [Internet]. [cited 2023 Nov 11]. Available from: https://www.bible.com/bible/97/1PE.4.12.MSG

10. Les Brown - My Life Story .. [Internet]. 2018 [cited 2023 Nov 11]. Available from: https://www.youtube.com/watch?v=7hAqvqM-Rqs

11. Les Brown Story of Persistence and Preperation – Ty Bennett [Internet]. [cited 2023 Nov 11]. Available from: https://tybennett.com/les-brown-story-of-persistence-and-preperation/

12. R. U. Darby « The Dream Ladder [Internet]. [cited 2023 Nov 11]. Available from: https://dreamladderblog.wordpress.com/tag/r-u-darby/

13. Numbers 14:28 Say to them, 'As I live,' says the LORD, 'just as you have spoken in My hearing, so I will do to you | New King James Version (NKJV) | Download The Bible App Now [Internet]. [cited 2023 Nov 11]. Available from: https://www.bible.com/bible/114/NUM.14.28.NKJV

14. Genesis 21:18 Go to him and comfort him, for I will make a great nation from his descendants." | New Living Translation (NLT) | Download The

Bible App Now [Internet]. [cited 2023 Nov 11]. Available from: https://www.bible.com/bible/116/GEN.21.18.NLT

15. Proverbs 4:23 Keep your heart with all diligence, For out of it spring the issues of life. | New King James Version (NKJV) | Download The Bible App Now [Internet]. [cited 2023 Nov 11]. Available from: https://www.bible.com/bible/114/PRO.4.23.NKJV

16. Proverbs 4:23 Guard your heart above all else, for it determines the course of your life. | New Living Translation (NLT) | Download The Bible App Now [Internet]. [cited 2023 Nov 11]. Available from: https://www.bible.com/bible/116/PRO.4.23.NLT

17. Investopedia [Internet]. [cited 2023 Nov 11]. 10 Business Audiobooks to Listen to on Your Commute. Available from: https://www.investopedia.com/articles/personal-finance/110915/7-business-audiobooks-listen-your-commute.asp

18. Moderate exercise: No pain, big gains - Harvard Health [Internet]. [cited 2023 Nov 11]. Available from: https://www.health.harvard.edu/newsletter_article/Moderate_exercise_No_pain_big_gains

19.	Sackton L. 8 Under 8: The Best Audiobooks Under 8 Hours [Internet]. BOOK RIOT. 2020 [cited 2023 Nov 11]. Available from: https://bookriot.com/audiobooks-under-8-hours/

20.	The Scotsman [Internet]. 2003 [cited 2023 Nov 11]. The JK Rowling story. Available from: https://www.scotsman.com/arts-and-culture/books/the-jk-rowling-story-2478095

21.	Ecclesiastes 3:2 A time to be born and a time to die. A time to plant and a time to harvest. | New Living Translation (NLT) | Download The Bible App Now [Internet]. [cited 2023 Nov 11]. Available from: https://www.bible.com/bible/116/ECC.3.2.NLT

22.	Proverbs 30:25 The ants are a people not strong, Yet they prepare their food in the summer | New King James Version (NKJV) | Download The Bible App Now [Internet]. [cited 2023 Nov 11]. Available from: https://www.bible.com/bible/114/PRO.30.25.NKJV

23.	Proverbs 6:6 Go to the ant, you sluggard! Consider her ways and be wise | New King James Version (NKJV) | Download The Bible App Now [Internet]. [cited 2023 Nov 11]. Available from: https://www.bible.com/bible/114/PRO.6.6.NKJV

24.	Acts 8:31 And he said, "How can I, unless someone guides me?" And he asked Philip to come up and sit with him. | New King James Version (NKJV) | Download The Bible App Now [Internet]. [cited 2023 Nov 11]. Available from: https://www.bible.com/bible/114/ACT.8.31.NKJV